A WORLD PARISH?

mchrist@drew.edu.

A World Parish?

Hopes and Challenges of
The United Methodist Church

Bruce W. Robbins

Abingdon Press
Nashville

A WORLD PARISH?
HOPES AND CHALLENGES OF THE UNITED METHODIST CHURCH

Copyright © 2004 by Abingdon Press

This book is printed on acid-free elemental-chlorine–free paper.

Library of Congress Cataloging-in-Publication Data

Robbins, Bruce. A world parish? : hopes and challenges of the United Methodist Church / Bruce W. Robbins. p. cm.
Includes bibliographical references and index. ISBN 0-687-00141-2 (alk. paper)
1. United Methodist Church (U.S.) I. Title.

BX8382.2.R63 2004
287'.6—dc22

2003022379

All scripture quotations, unless otherwise noted, are from the *New Revised Standard Version of the Bible,* copyright 1989, by the Division of Christian Education of the National Council of the Churches of Christ in the United States of America. Used by permission. All rights reserved.

06 07 08 09 10 11 12 13—10 9 8 7 6 5 4 3 2

MANUFACTURED IN THE UNITED STATES OF AMERICA

Contents

Acknowledgments

I appreciate so many who helped with the writing of this book. I first developed a paper for the directors of the General Commission on Christian Unity and Interreligious Concerns (GCCUIC) that I presented in October 2002. Bishop Walter Klaiber and others gave substantive responses that helped me develop the paper into a book. I am thankful to Bishop David Lawson for his reflections in response to a first draft of the present text.

I am also grateful to the staff of GCCUIC for their patience and willing acceptance of additional work as I sought to find time to write. Finally, thanks to my wife and children for their agreeable tolerance of a husband and father who was even more than usually wrapped up in his work and ministry.

Introduction

In November, 1990 I went to my first meeting of the Council of Bishops of the United Methodist Church in Jackson, Mississippi. I had just been elected general secretary of the General Commission on Christian Unity and Interreligious Concerns (GCCUIC). One of the responsibilities that the position carries is to provide staff support for the Council of Bishops on ecumenical matters. Having been a staff member of GCCUIC for four years, I had some idea of what were the ecumenical concerns of the church. But now I was in the more intimidating centers of power. As I think back, more than a dozen years later, that meeting began my excitement and alarm over what we call "the global nature" of the United Methodist Church.

A committee on the "Global Nature of the Church" had been meeting for several years in hopes of developing a recommmendation for a future general conference. That meeting in Jackson was the first time that the group had reported to the Council of Bishops. The committee presented material to a joint meeting of two of the Standing Committees of the Council: Relational Concerns and Teaching Concerns. The report envisioned a United Methodism separated into five regions of the world: United States, Europe, Africa, Asia, and Latin America. In terms of Latin America, they were envisioning that the independent Methodist churches of Latin America would "re-join" The United Methodist Church. (At that time, there were no United Methodists in Latin America. All of them had chosen and then been granted independence by General Conference. Since 1991 there have been United Methodists in Europe, many more in Africa, and a large group in the Philippines. In the last couple of years, United Methodist congregations and communities have begun in Honduras, Colombia, Vietnam, Cambodia, Nepal, and some other countries.)

I was both excited and alarmed by the global nature report. The excitement burst forth from the enthusiasm of the bishops wanting U.S. United Methodists to be in connection with sisters and brothers across the world by breaking down the barriers between us. Yet, I was also alarmed because the UM bishops were making plans for people from other churches and had not even talked with them! None of the Latin American churches that would make up a region were part of the discussion. Some bishops knew that some informal conversations were occurring through visits to the various churches. Others just assumed the Latin Americans would want to be part of a church with United Methodists again. Soon thereafter the bishops acknowledged the need for conversation and acted upon it. I drafted a letter on their behalf that went out to the autonomous churches.

That meeting was one of many meetings across many decades about the best international structure for the UMC. Understanding that history and the present challenges are both critical to decisions about where we wish to go in the future. To put it another way, understanding our past and present context may help us to discern better how God may be calling us to be a church in the twenty-first century.

Already, I am using two different words, international and global, to mean nearly the same thing, that is, the sense of The United Methodist Church extending beyond the United States. The term "global church" is sometimes used thoughtlessly within the denomination to apply *only* to United Methodism. That is a problem in itself, given that the UMC is less than one-half of one percent of global Christianity! The term "global United Methodist Church" is problematic as well. The UMC is not in all parts of the world. For that reason, I have used "international" instead of "global" from time to time. However, the term "international" isn't much better. Why should we organize our descriptions of Christianity across the globe using the political philosophy of a nation state? When United Methodists in one country relate to United Methodists in another country, the relationship is not primarily international, meaning *between* nations. The relationship is between people. Nations often have nothing to do with it and are even an impediment to the conversation. Unfortunately, there is no adequate term. So I use both terms with some sensitivity to the context of its use, while trying not to use the phrase "global church" when I mean United Methodism among different nations or peoples.

A Problem and a Gift

Before launching into the details of the present situation, two further thoughts may help.

A Problem

One of the great challenges of any global structure occurs when the whole contains parts with deep differences among them. Relationships between United Methodists in the United States and Africa, for example, are affected by the difference in wealth between the two places. Denominational leaders have not talked much about finances because of the sensitivity of the topic, but we can no longer avoid it.

My job places me in close relationship to the bishops of the UMC. I have watched in recent years as many bishops of the Central Conferences (those outside the U.S.) have advocated for salaries equal to bishops' salaries in the United States. With racism and paternalism so deeply imbedded in our system, the request carries strong weight with it. When speaking to an African bishop three years ago I asked, "Why do you need to have such a large salary when the cost of living of your nation is so low?" He replied, "A bishop in my country is like a king. And a king needs to give gifts, that is, to have things to give to his people."

I was struck by his complete and straightforward honesty with me. At the same time, I was deeply troubled about what this said about the church. What did it mean that a bishop received a salary for this reason, a salary that was many, many times greater than the few dollars per year that pastors in his area would receive? What did it mean that the church used this measure to provide aid to United Methodists? I did not know how to respond to this kind and honest bishop. I could not criticize his desire to help his people. At the same time, I could never agree with this model of the church. After putting on my ecumenical hat, I asked what the large salary would mean in this bishop's relationship with the other bishops in his city.

A Gift

It is a precious gift to see the global nature of the church lived out among United Methodists. Many Annual Conference teams have visited countries and hosted visitors from countries such as Zaire, Mozambique, the Philippines, and Colombia. To see the face of the world church as it is lived out or to hear stories about it is thrilling. We feel God's presence among us. And we see the needs: the need for spiritual renewal and the need for basic necessities in poverty-stricken and war-torn places. Such opportunities help us grow in knowledge and faith.

Of course, the visitors do not have to be United Methodist! But when they are United Methodist, the family connections are strong. Somehow it is different when people call themselves United Methodists, when they are us! Such is the gift the global United Methodist Church offers us.

The Purpose of This Book

During the past twelve years that I have had the opportunity to view The United Methodist Church in its relations with other churches, the UMC has been thinking hard about the church globally but has not made progress. Too many underlying considerations break upon the surface and stop the discussion. There are so many trees that it is hard to see the forest, whether that forest is the UMC or the Christian church. There are few places to turn for good information. Apart from the general conference reports themselves, very little has been written.

Because of the challenge to see the bigger picture and the urgency to do something about it, I have written this "primer" to present the "bigger picture" of the global church and the possibilities that await us. I offer my conviction that our present structure is inadequate to take us where we want to go as United Methodists. Since 1928, speeches have been made at General Conference calling for change. For some good and bad reasons the church has chosen not to change. Yet today, we reach a point of no choice. Our current infrastructure is unable to carry the weight of a truly just and sustainable "global church." We shall be unsatisfied with anything less. Now is the time to create a new structure for a global church.

Two principles seem paramount as we try to understand our denomination in terms of its global configurations. Both principles are vital for our integrity and faithfulness.

First, the *Book of Discipline 2000* says, "The heart of Christian ministry is Christ's ministry of outreaching love" (¶ 125). Our ministry as a community of faithful people called Methodists is to express the mind and mission of Christ. Such a bond can prevail over all the tensions mentioned here.

Second, we need openness. The world is fast changing and a new, flexible, adaptable structure is needed for United Methodists to be effective disciples to the world.

This picture of United Methodism comes to you through only one set of eyes—and mine are as limited as anyone else's! Other people have different points of view, especially those who live in the Central Conferences or have worked in them. I hope others will write what they see so that those interested can have a bigger picture than any one person can offer. Here is my attempt to give the best view that I can. I have heard the discussions in many places: at each Council of Bishops meeting since 1990, in the General Council on Ministries, and in ecumenical organizations. My work has also provided opportunity to visit many churches across the world.

An Outline for This Book

Chapter 1 begins with a description of our present circumstance—what our church is like in relation to other churches in the United States and across the world.

Chapter 2 asks, Who are we as United Methodists? Our tradition is one among many other great church traditions. Ecumenical institutions like the World Council of Churches (WCC) make it easy to compare who we are and what we do to our sisters and brothers who live and serve in other denominations. How do we look to ourselves and to others in this world? How does our self-understanding compare to the self-understanding of those who surround us? What can we learn from the comparison about what is most important to us?

In chapter 3, I will describe where we have been as a "global church." It will help us see more clearly where we want to go. United Methodists have made a remarkable journey. Although most of us are in the United States, many are in Africa, Europe, or Asia. There are also many Methodists who left United Methodism to form their own

Methodist or United churches in countries across the world. Others have left or been pushed out of Methodist churches to begin new churches, which happened with the Pentecostals. We know that Jesus calls us to be one in spirit with one another, if not one organizationally as well! How do we interpret and act upon God's call locally and globally (or decide when something is not God's call)? Our history is connected to our calling today. The call is to find the most effective, grace-filled ways in our unique circumstances to preach Christ to a broken world.

Chapter 4 addresses the considerable challenges we face. Most likely, every Sunday when we go to church we hear of needs somewhere, be it in our local community or somewhere far across the world. At the heart of our calling as United Methodists is to organize—to get *methodical*—in finding the best ways to respond and give witness to our faith. The "global nature" questions emerge today from many years of discussion about faithful discipleship as people called Methodists. The discussions are going on for so long and our progress is somewhat slow because the challenges we face are so vast! United Methodists do not have a distinct identity that clearly separates them from the wider Wesleyan family. Furthermore, enormous economic disparity exists between United Methodists in the United States and United Methodists in Angola or the Philippines. Too many times we are even competing with other Methodists and demonstrating to the world a divided rather than a united Methodism. Some people claim today that we need to guarantee through legislation and church courts that United Methodists agree on certain principles. Others claim that if we love and respect each other, that is connection enough.

Finally, in chapter 5, I present some alternative ways we can go forward as a denomination. The choices that our Church makes depend upon what we hold dearest and where we draw the dividing lines between those "in connection" and those outside of the connection. One challenge is to acknowledge the cultural differences of the places and societies where we live. In some places our bishops are regarded as servants who enable the pastors in the conference, while in other places they can be regarded as kings. There might be a big difference between those models. At the same time, we try to develop visions and theologies that tie them together, like the model of *servant leadership*. I will give some alternative models and suggest which ones fit us best for the future and for the vision we hold before us.

CHAPTER ONE

Our Present Circumstance

Before discussing in considerable detail what it means to be a member and citizen of The United Methodist Church, I shall draw a brief picture of our present circumstance. It is clear that the structure needs fixing and that the denomination has spent enormous amounts of money trying to fix it. The last general conferences demonstrated the need for change and also the difficulty in achieving change. At the heart of the dilemma is the following: many, many of us want to be part of a church that is global. We talk of our church as global and expect that it can be so. Yet, constantly, we come across barriers that challenge our initial perceptions. We have not begun to understand the consequences of the way we have chosen to live out the image we have of ourselves as a church.

Following are some glimpses of our life today that point to struggles involved in being a global church.

Central Conference Delegates

All United States United Methodists reside in jurisdictions, while all UMs outside the U.S. reside in Central Conferences. The number of delegates from Central Conferences has grown considerably at each General Conference. In 2004, 184 of the 994 voting delegates will be from the Central Conferences. The largest growth has occurred in Africa, and many of the delegates who come speak French or Portuguese but little English. However, until the 2004 General Conference, the UMC has published thousands of pages of reports—all in English. Plus there is little simultaneous translation in plenary and no translation in meetings of many of the subgroups of the conference. It seems as if the easy solution would be to translate documents and provide simultaneous translations in all settings. However, the cost for doing so is high, and it still does not address issues such as adequate distribution of documents, preparatory meetings, and so forth.

A deeper problem also exists that has not yet been addressed or even understood. Most of the work of General Conference involves amending *The Book of Discipline* and *The Book of Resolutions*. However, those books apply primarily to the jurisdictions and not to the Central Conferences. In fact, the vast part of most of the books can be set aside or amended at will within Central Conferences. The Central Conference delegates wonder at the dominant attention at General Conference to documents that do not directly affect them. At the same time, U.S. delegates get frustrated to see Central Conference delegates voting on issues that have nothing to do with them. Finally, the rest of the church wonders why there is no place for U.S. people to discuss U.S. issues! Every other country in United Methodism has such a place.

Agencies Trying to Be Global

Historically, only one of the agencies, The General Board of Global Ministries, related to the Central Conference United Methodists. However, since 1988, all of the general agencies have been expected to serve the *whole* church and not just the jurisdictions. However, this is impractical and nearly impossible for all except the four program boards (Discipleship, Higher Education and Ministry, Church and Society, and Global Ministries). During very recent times, when funding for the agencies has become tight, this fact has been articulated for the first time. The inability to serve the Central Conferences is articulated by all the agencies except for the Board of Global Ministries.

The "Elephant" of Huge, Financial Disparity

[handwritten annotation: Bishops travel cost to attend GC global general]

I call this an elephant because it is a powerful issue in the future of the church that few people understand or can address. And no one talks about it! Most United Methodists in the United States believe that all United Methodists pay into the connectional system through apportionments according to their ability to pay. However, Central Conferences do not pay apportionments and yet receive considerable resources of the church. Of course, in some places the needs are tremendous. Again, there is no place where plain conversation about the needs and resources can be openly discussed with equanimity. As the Central Conferences grow more rapidly than any part of the church, the demands upon the system need to be carefully understood.

The reality of the UMC structure is that patterns of dependence between the different parts of the church continue without an end in sight. The church by itself cannot counter the economic patterns existing between the developed worlds and developing worlds that only exacerbate the inequities. Central Conferences in Africa and Asia require grants and support to maintain not only the mission projects themselves but also the actual infrastructure that enables the "connection" to exist between the churches. The Central Conference bishops' biannual extended trips to the United States for Council of Bishops meetings (and continued travels in the United States to gather support for their areas) are just one example of the complex dependency that is a part of the actual infrastructure of the UMC.

One of the recent, idealistic goals—that of a global pension plan—may bring the tensions more directly to the surface. Right now, an interagency task force is beginning to propose a pension plan. Part of the funding comes from monies that have historically gone from the United Methodist Publishing House to the annual conferences in the United States. I suspect this reality is realized by few United Methodists. Many further questions will emerge that make clear the impossibility for the church and its resources to address the economic disparity that deeply affects the relationships. A pension plan may assist clergy dramatically, and it can rectify the disparity that now exists in compensation of bishops and clergy in many Central Conferences. However, what about the disparity that would then occur between the clergy and the laity in those annual conferences? The American United Methodists could never support a pension plan for all the laity as well as clergy.

Persons Wanting a New Relationship with the Current Structure

Leaders of the UMC face questions about who is part of the church, who is not, and whether there can be anything in between. Up to the present time, these questions concern the Central Conferences. Many persons in the Philippines wish that United Methodists in the Central Conferences could be more independent—"self-headed"—which means governing themselves. At the same time, others who are Methodist, but not United Methodist, want to be more formally part of the UM denomination (such as Methodists in the Ivory Coast). And then there is a third group: persons who were United Methodist and want to have some of the structural connections but with a greater degree of self-headedness than full membership allows. To make the situation more difficult, there aren't clear procedures or even places in which these discussions can occur.

Confusion over Structure Proposals

General Conferences have grappled with structure issues about the international makeup of the church for more than a century. Eighty years ago questions surrounded how much North American leadership would dominate other parts of the world: where would the bishops be elected? Today the debates seem more complicated. From 1996 until 2000, hundreds of thousands of dollars went into a proposal for a global conference and for new relationships. The proposal failed before the discussion even began at General Conference. People see the needs; they are simply not equipped to understand the issues. In light of the confusion, <u>hesitation</u> seems to be the better course. How can this change? *Hesitation for a century?*

Local and Global Tensions

In addition to finances and leadership questions, there are other tensions that are dominant and discussed extensively, formally and informally. One major question has to do with homosexuality. Do solutions to the conflict—our degree of acceptance or rejection of same-sex orientation and practice—need to be the same for all United Methodists? At this point, many United Methodists tend to think so. However, some Central Conferences exercise their right to change *The Book of Discipline* on this controversial issue. Should that be a possibility for jurisdictions as well? At present, most United Methodists do not think so. However, the debate may be affected by that issue.

Another Question and Challenge in the Future

If the church were able to shift its structure and direction it would be much better prepared to carry out its purpose to make disciples for Jesus Christ. At the same time, it would stand better able to engage in other critical discussions. I am thinking foremost of the challenge facing United Methodists by living in a multireligious world.

We are not prepared to encounter and seek to live peacefully with people from other faith communities. In the United States, many Muslims and Hindus live next door to us in rural as well as urban places. In Nigeria, United Methodists live in the midst of religious violence, intolerance, and tension with Muslims (sometimes the Christians being the intolerant ones). We need to learn what it means to be "good neighbors and good witnesses" as the General Conference calls us to be.[1] And we need to explore our own United Methodist theology. Does our doctrine leave space for respect and friendship with persons of other faith communities? I believe that it does. But, clearly, it is the topic for another important study. Our latest actions as a denomination show the need for new learning and decision making.

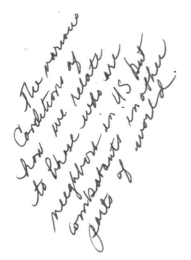

CHAPTER TWO

The Meaning of United Methodist Citizenship, Globally and Locally: Who Am I?

Being United Methodist is different from being Presbyterian or Roman Catholic or Quaker. Like many who read this, I have been a United Methodist since my baptism (although the word "United" wasn't part of the denomination's name at that time). I add the term "citizenship" to remind us of another dimension of membership: participation in the life and the society that exists around us wherever we live. We think of citizenship differently than we think of membership. One image is organic; the other is social. To be a "member" means to be an element, a component, or a constituent part of something, such as to be a member of the church or the Body of Christ. The term "membership" is at the heart of our theology. To be a "citizen" is to be a resident, a dweller, or an inhabitant in some particular place. For instance, I am a resident of the United States. But, more important, I am a resident of a local community in which the church is located. My membership in the church is *local* and *global* at the same time. I am a citizen in both places. Membership is organic; citizenship is social. Both are locatable in different kinds of entities. Sometimes the seemingly simple word becomes complicated. However, both concepts are important to understand.

The easiest way to describe what United Methodist citizenship means is to sort it out through a series of short sections that describe who a United Methodist is and some of the different views of identity that United Methodists hold.

I Am United Methodist

Technically, the United Methodist Church is delineated as comprising those persons who united from the Methodist Church and the Evangelical United Brethren Church in 1968. Those bodies were also the results of mergers of different groups dating back to the early years in American history. Generally, we can say that, from the Wesleyan tradition, United Methodism is the main branch that originated and developed from America out into the world.

The Methodist church began as a result of the mission outreach of John Wesley and the British Methodist societies. The beginning of the first division in the Wesleyan tradition came because of the American revolutionary war. After the war in 1784, American Methodism distanced itself from British Methodism when it held its first "Christmas conference" that established its structure independent of Britain and when it elected its own leadership.

The British Methodist Church and American Methodism engaged in mission and founded churches in many parts of the world. In British Methodism, the newly founded churches separated structurally from Britain, but they continued in close relationship with their mother church.

In American Methodism the pattern was different. Rather than remaining mission churches, many of the American overseas missions were organized into conferences and related to the UMC in the United States. The Liberia mission was the first conference external to the United States and it was established in 1832. From that point until today, there are new members added to the UM family through new congregational development in many different parts of

26

the world. (Of course, there were also many mission churches that did become independent.)

The UMC, as presently counted, includes the annual conferences, which are grouped into five jurisdictions within the United States. (The jurisdictions were created at the merger of northern and southern Methodist churches that had split over slavery in 1844. The 1939 merger created jurisdictions to provide some independence for the northern and sourthern portions of the new church.) The UMC also includes annual conferences in Africa, Asia, and Europe that are grouped into Central Conferences.

There is movement in and out of the UMC. The most recent example of persons joining the UMC from another tradition may be in Bermuda, where a number of congregations disaffiliated with the United Church of Canada and became part of the Baltimore-Washington Conference of the UMC. The most recent group to leave the UMC is the Methodist Church in Puerto Rico. The churches on that island petitioned General Conference in 1992 and received permission to become an "affiliated autonomous church"; however, they established a special relationship unique to them, which is discussed in chapter 4.

In addition to the structural relationships, to be United Methodist has a theological dimension. The UM heritage has doctrinal standards that set it apart from other churches. Those standards can be found in Part II of *The Book of Discipline 2000*. To be a United Methodist means to be in agreement with the doctrinal standards. Even though it is not fully clear, most United Methodists assume that this part of *The Book of Discipline 2000* should not be permitted to be changed by UMs in the Central Conferences.

Even with doctrinal standards, diversity of theological perspective is also upheld and celebrated within the denomination. What this means for the self-understanding of United Methodism can be challenging. One test may be to examine how those standards are used in consideration to both the maintenance of membership within the denomination as well as the standards for the admittance of new "churches" to become part of the UMC (such as the situation in the Ivory Coast as described in chapter 4 of this book).

The deeper question is the following: Does being United Methodist require adherence to specific doctrinal standards? And, at present, are those standards required for United Methodists in all parts of the world? Because of some present debates that are dividing the UM community, this question is not only important for the definition of "United Methodist," but it is a politically charged question that has bearing on all parts of the church.

Am I a Global United Methodist?

In general, United Methodists love to call themselves "global." Were we to start over, I would argue for us to abandon the term "global church." At the same time, I understand the appeal for us all to be part of the global church. We feel it more significant to be "global" than to acknowledge that United Methodism is only a small part of the Christian family!

Yet, the term "global" can sound presumptuous and self-aggrandizing, especially to those with an ear for ecumenical concerns. During the early parts of the twentieth century, the more common term used was "world church." But, like it or not, the term "global" is with us today, and good citizenship in the church and society requires us to think globally. Nearly all our actions have global consequences.

In one sense, we are global. United Methodists exist in many countries across the world including Africa, Asia, North America, and Europe. It is vital for us to keep the global perspective. Our lives and understandings are richer when we see through eyes other than our own local ones.

For many, the structural connection is vital to seeing through global eyes! However, we are also global through the Body of Christ. We can be taught by other Christians and other families as well as by our own. It is not a requirement for the fullness of our church (that is, the UMC) for the UMC itself to be the global church. In truth, we are a small part of a much larger whole.

Janice Love, a veteran ecumenist and international scholar, wrote an interesting essay concerning problems associated with the term "globalization" in relation to churches. She develops a typology of various kinds of churches or religious organizations.[1] The models go like this:

Global confessional model: Churches in this model have a vast geographic reach and a genuinely global organization. *R.C.* These churches are in virtually all regions of the world and draw people together on the basis of particular historic confessions. She lists the Roman Catholic Church, the Ecumenical Patriarchate of Constantinople (Eastern Orthodox tradition), and perhaps some confessional bodies that are groups of churches such as the Lutheran World Federation and the World Methodist Council as examples of this model. *GREATER BODIES OF COUNCILS OF CHURCHES*

Global inter-confessional model: "These Christian organizations stretch across all regions and most countries of the world and put Christians of many different doctrinal identities together in one organization." The primary example is the World Council of Churches, but the model would also include the World Evangelical Fellowship and the Old Catholic Church. The need for doctrinal agreement is less significant in this model.

Extended-national confessional model: "This model provides for a particular doctrinal tradition embodied in members primarily in one country, with additional churches in other nations or regions (hence the characterizations as extended-

UM is our extension of U.S. not really global (handwritten margin note)

national rather than global)." Here is where she places The United Methodist Church as well as some other U.S. churches. Some Orthodox churches, such as the Romanian or Ethiopian Orthodox Churches, would also be in this category.

Regional confessional model: This category includes churches of a particular doctrinal identity within a specific region, such as the Kimbanguist Church in Central Africa.

Regional inter-confessional model: This model includes Christian organizations within a particular region that are not linked by a particular confession or doctrine. Another name commonly used for them is Regional Ecumenical Organizations. One example is the All Africa Council of Churches.

1) distribution of members 2) nature of doctrine (handwritten margin note)

Two criteria stand out in the typology she develops: the extent of the distribution of the members, and the particular nature of the doctrinal tradition that connects them. As we saw, she labels the UMC as an "Extended-National Confessional" organization. The title better describes the statistical reality of the UMC in the present day than does "global church." As we shall see, both criteria are worthy of discussion in relation to the UMC. Janice Love argues that the UMC is not "global confessional" because of the geographical location of United Methodists. Were the membership far more widely spread out she might place it in the "global confessional" category. I ask whether the differences in theological beliefs within United Methodism might be such that the UMC, with a more widespread membership, might move into the "global inter-confessional" category rather than the "global confessional." Increasingly, there is less "particular historic confession" that distinguishes United Methodists from other members of the Wesleyan tradition who are found in the World Methodist Council.

In answer to the question, we are a global church if that means having members in different parts of the globe. However, we are not a global church as a religious community that has a visible presence in all regions and all continents, as does the Roman Catholic Church.

Am I an American Methodist?

Could every United Methodist answer this question positively? A quick response might be, "Of course not!" How could the thousands of United Methodists in North Katanga province of Zaire say, "I am an American Methodist"? Well, maybe their bishop does go to the United States twice a year for extended stays to attend the Council of Bishops meeting. Maybe they have heard that their clergy might be added to a pension fund based in Illinois. But they have never been to the U.S. How can they be American Methodists?

The question gets to the heart of United Methodist identity. Unlike British Methodism, the UMC has had the tradition of "intentional globality." That is, United Methodists have not forced new UM churches in different parts of the world to become self-governing. Despite pressure to the contrary, many American Methodist missions stayed with the mother church. Even though their Christian sisters and brothers may have suggested they follow a "colonial" or a "dependency" model, they have chosen this path. After all, the Roman Catholics have a structural connection to Rome.

Another way to answer the question is to say that American Methodists are clearly *not* British Methodists. Since the beginning these have been the two families of Methodism. And they are different from one another. For instance, British Methodists have never had bishops even though some churches that emerged from Britain adopted the practice (more than the theology) of an episcopacy. Further on in this journey of understanding Methodism, we will have to ask if the differences are great enough to see United Methodists as thoroughly different from other forms of Methodism.

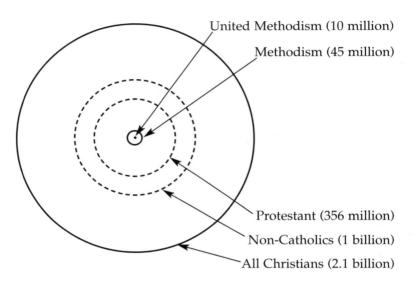

United Methodism (10 million)

Methodism (45 million)

Protestant (356 million)

Non-Catholics (1 billion)

All Christians (2.1 billion)

Notice the concentric circles with United Methodists in the center. United Methodists are such a tiny part of the body of Christians worldwide! Where should the circular lines be darker, or mark more of a barrier: between United Methodists and other Methodists, or between Methodists and other Protestants? As we shall see, the answer to that question will influence which models United Methodists could choose for its structure within the larger Christian and global community. I am convinced that the more appropriate distinction is between Methodists and other Protestants, not between United Methodists and other Methodists.

Before leaving this topic of "American Methodism," we need to see who is United Methodist but not "American" by national citizenship. Under the present structure the UMC has five jurisdictions within the United States and eighteen Central Conferences outside the United States located in Europe, Africa, and Asia. In chapter 3 we will explore how those conferences came into being. As of 2002, approximately eight million members live within the United States and two million members outside of it. That number is declining slightly in the U.S. and increasing significantly in other countries, especially in Africa and Asia. The change in membership is one of the factors that require us to attend carefully to the global versus American church and the changes resulting from the shift.

Am I a Pan-Methodist?

Again, we ask who we are as United Methodists in relation to other Methodists. Technically, the term "Pan-Methodist" includes all Methodists worldwide, such as those who are eligible to join the World Methodist Council, an organization that has seventy-one member churches.[2] These are churches whose lineage dates back to the Wesley brothers, or who have associated formally with that lineage. Some Pan-Methodists do not use the term "Methodist." For example, the Church of the Nazarene joined the World Methodist Council several years ago and recognizes that its roots stem from the Wesleyan tradition. The same would be true of the Salvation Army. Many Pentecostal and Wesleyan Holiness churches are also Pan-Methodist. People from one tradition gathered together in an organization like the World Methodist Council are called a "confessional family." More recently, the preferred name is a "Christian World Communion." Other examples are the Lutheran World Federation, the World Alliance of Reformed Churches, or the Anglican Communion, is us.

We also use the term "Pan-Methodist" in the United States to describe the four main Methodist bodies: the UMC and the three African American denominations that separated from the mainstream of Methodism. All three emerged directly from the American Methodist movement because of the blight of racism within the church. The African Methodist Episcopal Church (AME) separated in 1787 in Philadelphia when Richard Allen suffered a racial incident during communion and walked out with some followers. The African Methodist Episcopal Zion Church (AMEZ) formed shortly thereafter for similar racial reasons in New York City. The Christian Methodist Episcopal Church (CME) was created in the southern part of the United States immediately after the Civil War, again for racial reasons. A dictionary defines "blight" as "something that impairs growth, withers hopes and ambitions, or impedes progress and prosperity."[3] When people are prevented from full participation in Holy Communion or are denied their rights of full, equal participation in the church for reasons having to do with race, that is a *blight* facing the denomination that needs to be eradicated.

In the year 2000 the UMC began a process of repentance for the racism toward the African Americans in those churches and toward the African Americans who stayed United Methodist with an Act of Repentance at its General Conference. It was the first such formal act in the history of the denomination and may be the first step in a journey toward racial wholeness and toward reconciliation.

In recent years, the bishops of these four churches have been meeting together as a consultation of Methodist bishops. Any one of those bishops would likely say that God does not want us to be in separate churches. However, many fear that precious traditions could be lost through merger. In 1996 the bishops organized a call for a Commission on Union to be brought to all their general conferences. The UMC General Conference adopted the call in 1996 and provided funding for this commission. The other churches adopted and supported it as well. The development of the Act of Repentance was a way to help United Methodists learn the stories of separation and prepare for union.

However, that call was premature. The African American Methodist churches imagined how their traditions could be lost by joining the bigger church. In 2000, the work toward union was again linked structurally to cooperation, and a Commission on Pan-Methodist Cooperation and Union was formed.

Why is this story important to understanding the global nature of the UMC? How does this history influence our questions of UM citizenship? The answer has deep implications. As we shall see, there are two directions to look for greater visible unity among Methodists: you can focus locally and work together toward union with the Methodists nearest to you, such as the Pan-Methodists in the United States. Or you can look globally and see the structural connection with United Methodists in other parts of the world as primary because we are all part of the same church. But, is that fair when the blight of racism is what first divided Methodists in the United States? There is no easy answer. An ideal may be to find a structure that recognizes the historical and geographic bond with the African Methodist Episcopal, African Methodist Episcopal Zion, and Christian Methodist Episcopal churches, and makes that bond equivalent to our relationship to United Methodists in Central Conferences.

Presently, United Methodists work in two directions. First, we affirm our connection to United Methodists in other parts of the world. We do this more strongly than we affirm the connection to Pan-Methodists within the United States. We have done so since 1972. At the same time, we discuss union in the United States with these Pan-Methodist churches. Is there a way that we can find a structure that can affirm both relationships, structurally and theologically? Clearly, we are not there yet. In some places of the world, such as Angola, there are large tensions as well as competition between the UMC and another Pan-Methodist church, in this case, the African Methodist

Episcopal Zion Church (AMEZ). Angolan United Methodists were angry when AMEZ Methodists took some of their church property and switched the churches' denominational affiliation. When the United Methodist bishops in the United States sought to have conversations with their counterpart AMEZ bishops, it was not easy, nor did the churches talk easily about those relationships.

I Am Wesleyan

The affirmation that we are "Wesleyan" is related to being Pan-Methodist. Wesleyans are the followers of John and Charles Wesley, the people called Methodists. Historically, the British and American families went out across the globe because of their passion for mission, and we now have many millions of Wesleyans. The term is broader than Pan-Methodist since many Pentecostals would identify comfortably with this term.

The historical connection is only one part of what makes us Wesleyan. Far more important is the theological affinity! A section of *The Book of Discipline 2000* explains the "Distinctive Wesleyan Emphases" (pp. 45-48). Right before this section is another section that reads "Our Distinctive Heritage as United Methodists," but nothing in that section is distinctive of United Methodists that does not apply to all Wesleyans! The *Discipline* says:

> The Wesleyan emphasis upon the Christian life—faith and love put into practice—has been the hallmark of those traditions now incorporated into The United Methodist Church. The distinctive shape of the Wesleyan theological heritage can be seen in a constellation of doctrinal emphases that display the creating, redeeming, and sanctifying activity of God.

The text goes on to outline the power of grace in the Wesleyan tradition. It explains the powerful connection of faith and good works that sustains the passion for mission and service among Wesleyans. Here is one famous sentence that incorporates Wesleyan tradition: "For Wesley there is no religion but social religion, no holiness but social holiness" (p. 48).

United Methodists share these characteristics with Wesleyans the world over. When people hear the term "Methodist," I hope they will think of these kinds of commitments. Would that we could all live up to them! I am convinced that little difference exists between United Methodists and other Wesleyans. I envision a global church that places the special value of what it means to be Methodist within the wider Christian family.

Am I Protestant or Catholic?

Most United Methodists would answer "yes" to Protestantism without thinking very much about it. Generally, the term refers to those churches that separated from the Roman Catholic Church during the sixteenth century, following Martin Luther, John Calvin, and John Knox. Our heritage as Methodists is connected to the Church of England since John and Charles Wesley were priests in that church during the eighteenth century. The Church of England went through a reformation and separated from the Roman Catholic Church, although the separation was a mixture of political as well as religious motives. King Henry VIII of England wanted a divorce and the Pope would not give him one. So the Church of England parted ways with Rome. However, many people in Britain continued to be Roman Catholic or to feel theologically close to Rome.

In growing up, I never thought of myself as anything other than Protestant, and I think that most United Methodists also have always considered themselves Protestants. But, increasingly, Methodists are identifying with "catholic" tradition, that is, the church in its most global and historic sense. In some ways the catholic tradition is the Roman Catholic Church itself since more than half the world's Christians are Roman Catholic.[4] In other ways the "catholic church" is universal and the one "Church" that contains all Christians of the world. Not only do United Methodists today have a greater sense of the catholic tradition, but they have also moved closer to practices found in Roman Catholicism, such as the increased use of a lectionary of readings and a call for weekly Holy Communion. When I have traveled to foreign countries, I have found comfort in knowing that the Gospel lesson heard is the same one read in my local United Methodist Church in Vermont.

For years, many United Methodists have struggled with a phrase in the Apostles' Creed that says, "I believe in the holy catholic church." Even though the creed has a footnote saying that catholic means "universal" it is still a struggle for people. Maybe that will change as a result of the encouragement that comes through the ecumenical movement and people's realization that "catholic" is broader than "Roman Catholic."

Catholicity is one of the four "marks of the church" that Christians profess in the Nicene Creed when they say that we believe in the *"one holy catholic and apostolic church."* Catholicity describes the universality of the church. One World Council of Churches assembly described catholicity as "the quality by which the church expresses the fullness, the integrity and totality of life in Christ."[5]

Catholicity and globality can be similar in meaning. Both refer to a universality and breadth of vision that extends beyond borders or boundaries created by the human community. In his report to the WCC Central Committee in August 2002, His Holiness Aram I of the Armenian Apostolic Church, moderator of the Central Committee, compared globalization and catholicity. The comparison merits study, especially by Protestants in a nation like the United States that leads in globalization! For the moderator,

the grand difference lies in the way catholicity (unlike globalization) reinforces the authenticity of the local because of
its link, its connection, to the wider church. He writes:

CATHOLICITY

> Catholicity, unlike globalization, does not destroy the
> local; it does, however, reject the self-sufficiency of the
> local church and calls it to transform the exclusive and
> self-contained localism to inclusive and open locality.
> Catholicity is not universalization of the local church
> through universal structures. It is the God-given quality
> of church, which holds together universality and locality,
> and keeps the church growing and moving forward to
> God's future. (Report of the Moderator, Central
> Committee, August 2002)

The WCC moderator implies that the catholicity exists
locally and universally within the church of Jesus Christ,
not within a particular entity or segment of that church.
Were he to explicate this point, it would be extremely controversial within Orthodoxy. Similarly, it is pertinent to the
United Methodist understanding of the "global nature" of
the church.

We have

United Methodists, then, are both Protestant and catholic. Catholic.
In fact, the United Methodist General Conference has evangelical
affirmed that we are "Truly Catholic, Truly Evangelical, and
Truly Reformed" (*Book of Resolutions* 1988, p.174). That phrase
serves as a foundation for an ecumenical vision found in *The*
COCU Consensus that was adopted by the General reformed
Conference in 1988. All three of those words stand for vital tendencies
emphases within the Christian tradition. We know that
"catholic" means universal and is one of the marks of the
church found in the Nicene Creed ("the one, holy, catholic
and apostolic church"). To be evangelical represents hearing
and responding to the gospel's call to proclaim the word and
name of Jesus. To be reformed is to recognize the failure of
human beings to "get it right," and to be part of a church constantly "striving for perfection" (to use a Wesleyan phrase).

Am I Orthodox? *more conservative doctrine*

Until recently, the quick answer would have been "no." The Orthodox are those guys in the robes who stand during very lengthy services. Their Easter is even different from our own! After twenty-five years of relationship with Orthodox leaders in the World Council of Churches, I still find those relations the most difficult. Perhaps their lack of acceptance of me and of other Protestants is part of the struggle.

But, again, there is another side. Some scholars, usually to make a political point, are now referring to themselves as "orthodox Methodists." They want to let others know that they support the traditions of the church, usually in opposition to more liberal persons who weigh experience as equal to or greater than the criteria of Scripture or tradition on judging moral issues such as homosexuality. Technically, the word "orthodox" means praise (like doxology) of the straight doctrine or path. United Methodists who wish to reinforce this orientation call themselves orthodox.

I Am Connectional *does connection need to be within the system*

The Book of Discipline 2000 affirms that we are a connectional people. In the section on Wesleyan emphases that we examined earlier, it also says that United Methodists respond to the working of the Spirit "through a connectional polity based upon mutual responsiveness and accountability. Connectional ties bind us in faith and service in our global witness" (p. 48). Or, we are told that the "local church is a connectional society of persons" (p. 124).

Connectionalism is a unique gift that Methodists have to offer other parts of the Christian family. Historically, it has taken different forms. John Wesley uses the word to describe the relationship between the members of the Methodist society. In those cases it had a very particular meaning of someone holding membership in the society and someone under the supervision of John Wesley. In the years to come, its meaning was broadened significantly. Many United Methodists use the term to express the special relationship that exists between persons of that structure in different parts of the world. Bishop Nacpil, for example, has argued against autonomy for the Philippine United Methodists because if they became self-governing the "connection" would be broken. Others are convinced that connectionalism can be strong and vital between Methodists and other Christians even if they are not under the same governance authority. That difference of perspective becomes important in the search for the most appropriate structure for the UMC.

I Am Part of the Body of Christ

My personal ministry and special calling has revolved around a glimpse of the Body of Christ that I was given during part of my seminary training. My ministry has not been the same since. In 1975, I took a year's break from academic studies and began an intern year that took me to East Africa and to India. In Kenya I worked at my first meeting of the World Council of Churches. In India I joined a Roman Catholic religious order for six months, the Missionary Brothers of Charity. Both experiences taught me about the Body of Christ.

Further, I know of no gathering of Christians in the world that is more inclusive than an assembly of the World Council of Churches. A prayer circle can have an orthodox monk from the desert on one side of you and a Pentecostal from the heart of Mexico City on the other side. Perhaps the most famous symbol of the breadth of the Body is the sound of the Lord's Prayer when spoken in many different languages at the same time.

From these experiences I have learned both how small and how rich a part of world Christianity we comprise as United Methodists. I knew it to be small because I was so surrounded by people from other traditions. When I traveled globally, I knew that I could find a Roman Catholic church nearly anywhere—not so for a United Methodist church! The Body of Christ was large and all-encompassing. I was indeed part of it but a very small part.

Then I traveled to India and learned a different lesson about the Body of Christ. My time with the Missionaries of Charity was spent with very sick people. I would pick them up on the streets and carry them to the House for the Dying, or I would care for them in hospitals throughout Calcutta. The conditions were often difficult. I remember being asked to take care of one sick boy lying on a mat. I could not do it. A missionary brother named David went over and helped him in ways that I could not. Later on, I asked Brother David how he was able to care for the boy who was surrounded by all the filth. Brother David said it was easy: that was the Body of Christ lying there on the floor. The lesson? The Body of Christ incorporates and connects us all, no matter our condition. It sounds easy in retrospect, but it was a hard lesson to learn at the time.

From a Methodist point of view, the Body of Christ stretches across the world and includes all of humanity. As Paul writes, "For just as the body is one and has many members, and all the members of the body, though many, are one body, so it is with Christ" (1 Cor. 12:12). Through other passages and interpretations, the Body can incorporate the whole of creation. And the important lesson is the connection that exists among us. The difficult aspect is how we distinguish the Methodist family from the whole body. Do we emphasize the divisions within the body that our families represent? How many families should there be?

I Am Part of the Church Universal

The Book of Discipline 2000 is clear that the UMC is part of the church universal. It is so declared in the church's constitution: "The United Methodist Church is part of the church

Connect to the Body of Christ ecumenically + globally

universal, which is one Body in Christ" (¶ 4). Several other places also declare it so (¶ 101, p. 43; ¶ 203, etc.). The commonly held view is that anyone we call Christian is part of the Church, albeit in a different branch. For those from churches more exclusive in character, this ecumenical vision is considered a heresy. For us, as United Methodists, it is foundational to our beliefs. John Wesley emphasized this point in sermons such as the one on "The Catholic Spirit."

we are separated by our belief about sacrament ordination

During my ecumenical ministry, I have had to realize that this sensible view is not commonly held. When I began entering ecumenical circles in 1975, I struggled to understand how people could deny other Christians access to the communion table. I slowly learned that for many other Christians (even a majority), Holy Communion was an act that could only take place among those *completely* united in Christ. And it was obvious that we had differences among us, with the question of the ordination of women being prominent. In succeeding years, I learned how some churches, like the Russian Orthodox, would even question the validity of my baptism. For so many, the church universal is comprised of only the persons in their own church! The long tradition of the Roman Catholic Church, for example, equates the church universal with the Roman Catholic Church. Others of us—even those in dialogue with them— are seen by them as "ecclesial communities." United Methodists think their openness is the norm; rather, it is the exception—although common in the United States.

If you live in the United States, you may think of the UMC as a large church. It is one of the predominant Protestant churches in the U.S. with churches in most counties of the country. We even talk about "the church" and mean the UMC. But the perspective is quite different in Rome or Moscow or Geneva (home of the World Council of Churches). I remember being so surprised when Russian Orthodox colleagues in Moscow had trouble telling United Methodists from Jehovah's Witnesses. The Orthodox know the Catholics and even some Lutherans and Baptists. But Methodists? No. United Methodists in Europe are far more aware of the "smallness" of the UMC in contrast to other traditions.

Unlike the Orthodox, United Methodists do not see themselves as "the church." But they do sense themselves, at times, to be a "self-sufficient church," not needing the other branches and trunks of the Christian community— sometimes not even fully aware of their presence.

Comparable statistics about United Methodism within the Christian community are helpful. The UMC has approximately ten million members, one and a half million of whom live outside the United States.[6] Methodism worldwide, stemming from British and American missionary efforts, is more than four times greater than United Methodism with forty-four million members. Protestantism expands the concentric circles much farther; it is thirty-five times greater than United Methodism. And Christianity is more than two hundred times greater than United Methodism with roughly two billion adherents. The only church that can bear the name "global" with full integrity may be the Roman Catholic Church with its one billion members spread completely across the globe.[7]

Are We a Self-Satisfied Church?

After all these questions and discussions, we can place ourselves better in the global Christian community. We are a small but vital part of the breadth of Christianity that is miraculous in its scope and character. From twelve disciples sent out into the world we have a faith community that includes nearly half of humanity! And we, as United Methodists, are a part of that community. I am personally captured by the grandeur and biblical character of that vision of the church universal and my part within it.

Within this larger church, our perspective is very ecumenical and undergirded by the Constitution of the UMC.

are we too comfortable in our separations

We do recognize nearly all other Christians as belonging to the Christian church. (However, there are boundaries such as the recent refusal at General Conference to recognize Mormon baptism as Christian baptism.) Churches of the Protestant tradition do tend to recognize other churches more easily and readily than do some other church traditions (Orthodox, Catholic, or Pentecostal). Associated with this pattern in Protestantism seems to be an acceptance of the "brokenness" of the church. Today, many Protestants live quite contentedly, seeing themselves as one part of a church with many different "branches."[8]

In recent years, this perspective of a broken yet contented church has been challenged in both ecumenical and Methodist discussions. The following question has been repeatedly posed to churches of the Protestant tradition: *How does your church understand, maintain and express your belonging to "the one holy catholic and apostolic church?* (At the same time, the Orthodox churches have been asked, *Is there space for other churches in Orthodox ecclesiology?* The question is very pertinent to Orthodox/United Methodist relationships especially in Russia today.)[9] The question to Protestants is important to consider within the discussion of the "global nature" of the church. Where should the denominational lines be that divide Christians from one another? And why do we have them? Is there a way for a "local church" to also understand itself as "catholic"? We could mean by "local" what the Roman Catholics mean: a collection of churches within a nation or region. And by "catholic" we can mean "universal," or those churches in connection with one another through the theological vision of the Body of Christ.

I encounter too often a darker side to our self-understanding as United Methodists. Some say, "Why do we need to work with other Christians? Our divisions are because we have different preferences and desires. We have plenty to do within our own church." The excitement of meeting other United Methodists across the world makes us think that we do not need other Christians. They do their ministry and we do ours. Sadly, such a view ignores Jesus' call to oneness. The view also avoids the enormous pain caused in many places because of self-satisfaction. Can we remember that even if we cannot see the vision of one church, God may still be holding it before us? By working within us, God may be able to accomplish far more than we ourselves can ever imagine (Ephesians 3:20).

where is
the need for
"oneness"

Our Historic Journey to the Twenty-first Century: A United Methodist Church with Members on Several Continents

Historical Perspective   *Liberia first*

Since 1832, The United Methodist Church, or a predecessor body, has been a global Methodist church. The Liberia Mission Annual Conference became the first conference external to the territory of the United States. For many years it was served from the United States with leadership elected by the General Conference and sent to Liberia. This relationship was the first of many missions whose work came to be the heart of Methodism. More than anything else, theological or historic, we <u>Methodists are a people on a mission</u>. The nineteenth century saw the empowerment and establishment of the Methodist Church in America. The excitement and enthusiasm of the Methodists led to extensive openings of mission work throughout the world. Sadly, the work was less than it could have been because of the dividedness of American Methodism between the Methodist churches of the South and the North.

My purpose in this section is to catch glimpses of two pivotal, historic moments in the United Methodist search for an authentic institutional structure for the church. Not surprisingly, many of the issues from one time and context are similar to a different context many years later. The first historical moment is the General Conference of 1928 when the Central Conference structure was created. The second moment comes in 1968 with the report of the Commission on the Status of Methodism Overseas to the General Conference. With those historical insights in mind, I will turn in the following chapter to the present time. I believe it is another pivotal time for change. We as a denomination have been patiently stumbling, seeking a vision of a new direction. Perhaps now is the time!

The Revolutionary Acts of General Conference 1928

In 1928, the General Conference of the Methodist Episcopal Church took two steps that set a new direction for the mission work of the church. The changes seemed so significant at the time (and still do, in my opinion) that the 1932 General Conference report of the 1928 actions wrote about it in the following way:

> Of the action whereby the two constitutional amendments on Central Conferences were recommended by the General Conference in 1928 and afterwards adopted by overwhelming votes in both the Annual and Lay Electoral Conferences of the Church, one discerning Methodist leader declared it was "the most radical and at the same time the most conservative measure" taken in Methodism in the past 100 years. These amendments were radical in that they represented a marked change in the policy and organization of the Church and conservative in the sense that they brought to the sons of Wesley in so-called foreign lands a new insight into the generous spirit of Methodism and the meaning of Christian brotherhood and a new appreciation and respect for the Church as an instrument intended primarily for the

Main purpose is building the kingdom!

upbuilding of the kingdom of God. (*Journal of the General Conference 1932*, p. 1438)

1) structure of Central conf.

What were these two changes? The first was to actually create the structure of Central Conferences. The second was to empower Central Conferences to elect their own bishops.

2) Empower CC to elect bishop

In addition to these actions, the General Conference also established a new Commission on Central Conferences. The Central Conferences and their coordinating body continued through the 1939 union and have since then been a structural part of the UMC.

Following the dramatic words quoted above, the report tried to analyze the pressures facing the Methodist Episcopal Church in terms of its foreign relationships. Reviewing that material today makes for fascinating reading since the pressures facing the church then are similar to those of today.

First, the notion of a new structure called "Central Conferences" was quite novel. Only the Methodist Episcopal Church created Central Conferences. Other churches, Methodist or otherwise, had no such structure. The Methodist Episcopal Church, South, and the Methodist Protestant Church had mission work, but the relationship and authority was directed by the mission agencies located within the United States. The establishment of a structure such as Central Conferences that sought equity and empowered the younger churches was remarkable for its day. In another place the 1932 report says that "the adoption of the new Central Conference legislation has sent a thrill throughout the whole Christian world" (*Journal of General Conference, 1932*, p. 1440).

Second, the mood was for further change. There was also the matter of Central Conferences choosing their own leadership. Prior to 1928, the leaders had been elected and sent out from the United States. The General Conference voted to allow for their election within their own regions. As noted above, constitutional changes had to go before the annual conferences for ratification before they could take effect. However, the excitement for change was so great that the first bishops were elected only three months after the Council of Bishops ratified the constitutional changes! On February 27, 1930, the Central Conference of Eastern Asia elected two bishops. Others were elected before the year was over. According to the 1932 report, the change made possible by General Conference created a "new dignity and self-respect as well as loyalty and devotion to Methodism and the work of the Kingdom." The adulation continued: "A new sense of human brotherhood has emerged and a new resolution to meet the high responsibilities of Christian discipleship has made itself felt in all these lands" (p. 1441).

Third, the Commission on Central Conferences reported on another remarkable change in the life of the world church relationships. Between the 1928 and 1932 General Conferences, two new church bodies formed: The Methodist Church of Korea and the Methodist Church of Mexico. Different pressures led to the establishment of these churches, but both of them were the result of merger of the Methodist Episcopal Church and the Methodist Episcopal Church, South. The desire for unification of Methodism came to fruition more quickly in these places than it did in the United States. The report doesn't state it, but the Methodist Church of Brazil also became autonomous at the same time.

Uniqueness of American Methodism

In addition to describing the historic moment and then recommending some small adjustments to the structure, the report in 1932 described the implications of the 1928 changes and what some new directions for the future might be. The commission was emphatic to say that it did not "presume to recommend the particular course that the General Conference should take." However, the commission did think that these three perspectives made American Methodism unique. They then gave three possible directions for the future.

First, here are the three perspectives:

The first perspective involves equity. The General Conference is unique among Protestant churches in the world because it is composed of representatives "from both the older and the younger churches on a basis of equality . . . there is not discrimination between delegates from the older churches at home and those from the younger Annual Conferences in foreign fields" (p. 1442).

equal representation at GC.

Not only did the commission celebrate this sense of equality, but it went on to express concern for a seeming inequality. The General Conference by constitution must meet in the United States, and this can create an appearance of being "controlled by the American base." The carefully nuanced language does not suggest moving the General Conference, but it does call for the "necessity of thinking afresh." It is a fascinating example of insightful thinking.

Meeting in US looks suspiciously unequal

The second perspective involves self-governance. The report acknowledges that "practically all other Protestant denominations, both in America and in Europe, have had the policy of setting up independent, self-governing churches from the beginning in their missionary activity." And those newly established churches have not had any official relationship with the mother church. That has been their fixed purpose, it repeats, "creating self-supporting, self-governing and self-propagating churches from the beginning . . . as quickly as possible." The report contrasts this "natural" pattern to the one of Methodists "to think of a centralized control of their far-flung church line." Again, the thinking is prescient, and we shall see this issue being key to the debates at the 1968 General Conference and in the life of the UMC even today.

self governance vs connectional

I am quite struck by the way the report seeks to present these different approaches without judgment as to which is

the best. As the report indicates, the American Methodists were using a pattern that was rejected by nearly every other Protestant church in the world: continuing the centralization from the mother church and not encouraging the three legs of what was called the Three-Self Movement—self-supporting, self-governing, and self-propagating churches.
~~*ecumenical came from mission churches*~~ tion would become more apparent by American Methodism also flew in the face of the assumed call of the world Church and the Body of Christ. The pathway this Methodist mother church was taking seemed unecumenical: "In any mission field of the world where the desire for church union has manifested itself strongly, observers will probably admit that the arrangement of the churches, other than Methodist, has made it simpler and easier for the younger churches to come together for discussion, mutual understanding and actual union" (p. 1443).

It is important to remember how strong the church union movement was at this time. The origins of the modern ecumenical movement emerged from the mission field. The dividedness of the Christian community and its hindrance to the unity of the Body of Christ was most apparent as the various Christian groups entered into competition with one another in the "field of the Lord." To create or perpetuate structures that impeded what so clearly seemed to be God's call was strongly challenged. Those on the commission must have been acutely aware of those pressures as they wrote the words quoted above. They note how Methodist churches in Japan, Mexico, and Korea were recently established "on the basis of union with other Methodist bodies," and that the American mother church had to take extraordinary steps to grant full autonomy to those younger churches before they could be united with their local Methodist sisters and brothers. (Remember, there were the Methodist Churches North and South, the Methodist

Protestant Church, as well as many other Methodist churches involved in mission work.)

Possible Directions for the Future

Finally, let us reflect on "three possible directions" posed by the Commission on Central Conferences as a result of the circumstances and the perspectives just listed. They also anticipate future debates and choices. Listen to the context in which the commission places the options: "In the light of the foregoing facts and the experiences of other denominations in handling the problems involved in the growing independence of the younger churches what further development of the Central Conference as an authoritative body for the government of Methodist Churches in any given territory may be expected?" (p. 1443).

1) Option One: "Central Conferences could be developed into independent Methodist churches. . . . For instance the Central Conference of Southern Asia could be set up as the General Conference of the Methodist Church of Southern Asia." This would sever all voting representation in the General Conference that meets in America. It goes on to say that such a separation "would not relieve, in any way, the missionary responsibility of the Mother Churches" and it would retain the relationships with America for those areas not ready for independence.

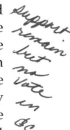

2) Option Two: This option is to "form a Central Conference here in the United States and then organize a General Conference with representatives from all of the Central Conferences." The General Conference would be a "small body" to deal with general problems and to maintain relationships with other Methodists and international church organizations worldwide. The advantages of this plan are summarized: "This plan would provide for the measure of self-government which seems to be necessary in the present stage of the world's life, would prevent the churches from

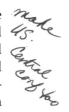

coming too much under the influence of nationalistic influences and would lay the basis for a true ecumenical Methodism" (p. 1444). The question of nationalism became another important issue in the debate during the seventy years to follow.

3)

remain in some connection

Option Three: The status quo is presented as the third option. "The present polity might be continued—keep the General Conference representative of all Annual Conferences, both at home and abroad, with dual voting in any Central Conference territory" (p. 1444). Central Conferences would continue as structures to enable mission, General Conference would deal mainly with U.S. affairs, complete autonomy would be granted to none, and the "final authority is with the General Conference which is predominantly American."

Conclusion: The commission's conclusion was the following: it is clear that the present situation calls for larger freedom and autonomy and that there is a "high obligation" to cooperate in union movements but that time is a factor and more transition is needed. Nevertheless, the final determination of the recommendations was the opinion of those from Central Conferences and this became the persuasive voice: "It should be noted that the sentiment registered in the Commission by the members from Central Conference territories was unanimous that, for the present, a world-wide Church, centering in the General Conference as we know it, is the form of organization best adapted to the situation" (p. 1445).

In years to come, there would be criticism within the Central Conferences of their leaders. Concerning those who support the status quo, are not they the same persons who have the opportunity to go to the United States and to take advantage of the opportunities created by the "world church"? It is fascinating to read between the lines about the quandary faced by the American members of the commission. They saw the impediments and the concern expressed by other parts of the world Church beyond Methodism. They tried to articulate it in the report (in terms of both self-governance and barriers to union). Yet, they felt it most important to listen to the voices of the leadership from the Central Conferences who sat around the table with them. Otherwise, they would be exercising a paternalism far more concrete than the structural paternalism inherent in the present church structure. It was a conundrum that would pass from one General Conference to another up to the present day.

The Debates and Possibilities at the 1968, 1970, and 1972 General Conferences

The pressures articulated in the 1932 General Conference report, especially the movement toward autonomy, required considerable study within the denomination and a continued search for a new pattern of relationships. Churches that did become autonomous—such as the churches of Brazil, Korea, and Mexico—wanted deeply to remain in close relationship with the American "mother church." In fact they hoped that their relationships (especially the financial support that they received) would remain as strong as they ever were as Central Conferences. Promises were made to many of them that this would be true.

With new, autonomous churches blessed and sent into new life by the General Conference, and with the continuation of Central Conferences, the denomination struggled to find new ways of relationship and to reconcile the ones that they had. Many people saw the need for study and attention to the global relationships. Of course the reflection was secondary to other huge issues that faced Methodism during these years, such as the discussions that led to the 1939 union of the Methodist Episcopal Church and the Methodist Episcopal Church South. The decisions in that merger included the continuation of the Central Conference structure as well as powerful relationships with the affiliated autonomous churches. After the reunion, the discussion—as were almost all discussions—was set aside because of the world war.

However, the structural discussion came to the fore once again at the 1948 General Conference. At that time, the conference established what came to be called COSMOS, the Commission on the Structure of Methodism Overseas. The 1948 General Conference created this commission to be independent of the Board of Missions. It was, however, aided extensively by the staff from that Board.

For this discussion, we enter COSMOS's life through the major report it gave to the 1968 General Conference. The years between its creation and 1968 were filled with political changes that affected what became The United Methodist Church in 1968. Political changes such as the powerful force of political independence movements, the challenge to the pervasive pattern of colonialism, and the international hope and passion for solidarity centered on the United Nations that was also created at the closing of World War II. The importance and influence of the discussions that culminated at the 1968 General Conference were somewhat veiled by the celebration of the new denomination's creation. At the same time, considerable floor time was given to speakers to support the proposals from COSMOS. The commission believed that it was a crucial time for decision making in the life of the newly forming church.

The COSMOS Report

The report to the General Conference is extensive: it summarizes the previous quadrennium and brings a myriad of requests for continuation of the status quo for some churches and autonomy for others. Then it presents "Proposals for the Future" that caused considerable debate. The review of the past quadrennium told about the 1964 General Conference mandate to study the church structure and make recommendations. It carried this mandate out through consultations in all jurisdictions and Central

Conferences and through one large mission consultation (Green Lake, 1966). The renewal and autonomy requests were extensive with twenty-five conferences seeking autonomy, many more than all the combined requests of previous years. The recommendations weren't noteworthy in themselves, but the committee explained their implications in an additional statement to the conference. The recommendations were:

1. To continue COSMOS,
2. To hold jurisdictional meetings to report on the convictions of the commission that emerged from the Green Lake consultation, and
3. To hold a World Methodist Structure Congress to examine the issues of unity, autonomy and interdependence as they affect the UMC's world structure, and to consider the possibility of a new world structure that would have powers agreed upon by the constituting regional bodies (COSMOS would present a new structure to the next General Conference).

We shall focus on the presentation and debate on the last proposal. It carried the weight of COSMOS's desire. Eventually all three recommendations were adopted with slight amendment,[1] but, as we shall see, this discussion was the high water mark of the move to a new structure that favored autonomous bodies worldwide.

Presentation of the Proposal for a World Structure Congress

The committee said that "change in the present structure of world Methodist (sic) is desirable and necessary because":

1. There is tremendous growth of members outside the United States who want greater freedom to make decisions;

2. A new climate has been created by the spread of nationalism and by a desire for independence and self-determination;

3. All present structures are controlled by a General Conference whose membership is 90 percent from the United States and "whose time is devoted to concerns of the American church." It can't give proper consideration to the other forty-five countries of United Methodism;

4. The emergence of world and regional ecumenical councils raises questions as "to how Methodist groups should be related in these areas and be fully participatory in these bodies and at the same time under the jurisdiction of General Conference."

5. "A deepening conviction that to drift or make minor shifts in present structures is to decide against a world church by default." *(Change must take place)*

After presenting these reasons, the commission outlined the "developments and issues" behind these reasons. Then it called for seven speakers to convince the conference. By looking at these reasons and then hearing the speakers, we can sense the quandary that was faced in 1928 and 1932—the "fruitful tension" between autonomy, interdependence, and unity.

Explanation of the Tension

The additional reflective statement by COSMOS tells of the early days. Methodists felt the Spirit calling them "to send as many missionaries to as many countries as possible so that the world might be won for Christ." Experience showed the destructiveness of "competing denominations." The experience led to the desire and need for greater freedom, legislatively and administratively. Central *one problem - colonialism + its power*

Conferences were created to meet the initial calling. And the creation of autonomous churches was a response to the experience that followed. Five requests for autonomy in 1964 and twenty-five requests in 1968 are evidence of that. The weakness of the structure was presented in the report as follows:

> During our study, one who has lived and served abroad said that we are in reality not a world church in structure but an <u>American church with overseas outpost</u>s. The lines of authority and communication are almost exclusively from America to groups overseas. . . . If we are to be a world church with a world mission, our structure must reflect our nature and task. (*1968 General Conference Journal*, p. 92) TOP DOWN POWER

In order to respond to the pressures and tension, COSMOS made four structural suggestions for adjudication at the proposed World Methodist Structure Congress. The conference needed to decide between these four options. They are:

1. Make necessary changes to General *Change GC* Conference legislation but no major structural *not church structure* changes;
2. Urge Methodist groups outside the United States to become autonomous and form united churches;
3. Create a world Church with an <u>International General Conference.</u> There would be a common basis of "Faith ministry, membership and general episcopacy." The International General Conference would be confined to matters of international concern. There would be regional <u>General Conference</u>s. Each regional conference would write its own *Discipline* and hold all responsibility suited to its region.

4. Create a "World Conference of Methodist Churches which would consist of autonomous regional churches meeting together on a world level for primarily consultative purposes."

Green Lake Consultation

The report states that the consultation in Green Lake held two years earlier in 1966 considered all these recommendations but focused on the third and fourth as the ones the participants considered supporting. At the close of the consultation, their report to COSMOS recommended the fourth option. This would mean that the United States and the Central Conferences would all become regional conferences. The report goes on to say that the desire of COSMOS was to hold many conferences in the jurisdictions and the Central Conferences to discuss the reasons and options for change. But, because the Methodist and EUB reunion was "so immediate and vital," they postponed this plan and called for the regional conferences and the World Structure Congress for the years 1968–1972. With those comments, the report ended.

Plenary Discussion

Bishop Raines, chairperson of COSMOS, asked that the General Conference allow various speakers to make clear to the delegates the important need for the World Methodist Structure Congress. He received permission to invite seven persons to address the conference. Obviously, these discussions exceeded time limits and the conference had to find additional time for the report! All the speakers are instructive to us as we try to understand the trajectory of the global nature discussions in United Methodism. Here are relevant comments taken from the presentations (*1968 General Conference Journal*, pp. 243-50):

Bishop Barbieri (Buenos Aires Area, Central Conference) gave three compelling reasons for autonomy. (All Latin American Central Conferences were seeking autonomy.) The first is called today subsidiarity: "laws, regulations and structures have to be created as close as possible to the place where the decisions have to be made." He said: "We do not seek autonomy for autonomy sake; it is an autonomy for a better discharging of the mission in each place. The present General Conference is ... hardly fit to meet the needs of the whole world, not withstanding every good intention." Second, "autonomy does not intend to be a mere drifting away from each other, so as to become nationalistic and isolated units." In Latin America they are forming a regional Methodist body so that they can "try to preserve the fundamental characteristics of the Methodist tradition and genius." And finally they want to link the regional conference to a world conference. That is why he is advocating for the Structure Congress.

[handwritten margin notes: 1) ; GC cannot meet world's needs]

His summary statement of "autonomy within the interdependence and unity within diversity is our aim" was a powerful articulation of the vision of the World Conference. (Bishop Barbieri was vice-chairperson of COSMOS.)

Bishop Wilbur Smith (Methodist Church of Brazil) praised autonomy and the growth that resulted from it in Brazil. He also stated dissatisfaction that his church had to relate to the UMC through the Board of Missions instead of directly, that is, church to church.

Bishop Alejandro Ruiz (Methodist Church of Mexico) spoke of the way autonomy helped the church lift the burden, that people perceived the church to be beholden to the United States in the face of the fierce nationalism of Mexico. But he hoped for a stronger relation through a world conference. *[handwritten margin note: fear of U.S. Church]*

John Shaefer (former EUB tradition) spoke of the need for the churches together to address the emerging questions, stating that churches wanting autonomy "do not want to repudiate the family connections."

Bishop James K. Mathews (Boston Area) was president of the Consultation on Church Union (an American plan of church union referred to as COCU) and was asked how the proposed structure congress might affect the COCU discussions. On one hand, he said, we cannot "press too stoutly for a kind of pan-Wesleyanism" since it may well contradict the aims of COCU. Then he added: "On the other hand, if we understand the intention of COCU, to be the establishment of a purely national church in the United States, this should also do violence to the concept of the church universal."

Christian unity is based upon "oneness of all in each place" *and* a "unity in relationship also to the church in all other places—a basic emphasis of COSMOS," said Bishop Matthews. These two phases must be brought together in a "fruitful tension."

Bishop Odd Hagen (Northern Europe Region) said that the congress and proposed world conference need not conflict with the World Methodist Council and that the UMC must find its own structure.

After all these speeches there was limited debate. The resolutions passed easily. The funds for the jurisdictional visits were cut, but the World Structure Congress was authorized to proceed. # 4

The next General Conference mention of COSMOS and its proposals came in a brief report at the 1970 General Conference. Given the time and energy of the 1968 conference just reported to you, one would have guessed that there would be eager anticipation for the report. However, very little happened officially. The World Methodist Structure Congress had been held in Atlantic City just two weeks before the General Conference. The report and recommendations would come to General Conference in 1972. Other normal work occurred. A new Central Conference was created, and autonomy was granted to the Hong Kong Provisional Annual Conference. The report also mentioned that the jurisdictional conferences that had been called for in 1968 had taken place. That was it.

1972 General Conference

Remarkably, 1972 marked the end of COSMOS and all its proposals. The report authorized numerous episcopal elections in Central Conferences and recommended five new autonomous churches. Then it called for its own discontinuation and the creation of the Committee on Central Conference Affairs. It also called for a variety of other actions: the right of autonomous churches to communicate with the Council of Bishops, a new definition for affiliated autonomous churches, a call for the creation of concordats with all of them, and the addition of delegates from those churches to General Conferences.

The final comment of the report speaks loudly of the change that had occurred since 1932. As a result of all the consultations (jurisdictions, central conferences, affiliated autonomous churches, etc.) it read, "As a result of this process COSMOS recommends to the General Conference of the UMC that the World Methodist Council as presently structured become an adequate instrument for worldwide fellowship and cooperation of all the churches of the Methodist tradition."

From reading the reports, many questions remain. After all the insights and articulations of the need for change, the final acts of COSMOS were to recommend exactly what had been cited as a danger: small modifications that do not address the "fruitful tensions" facing the church. The forces supporting the vision of Central Conferences in the present arrangement had prevailed. Even though small improvements were made to the relationships with affiliated autonomous churches (e.g., direct communication with the

Council of Bishops, observer delegates to General Conference, the advocacy of concordats with autonomous churches), they would continue to struggle to find their place in any relationship with the UMC independent of the General Board of Global Ministries (new name for the Board of Missions). From that point on, small steps were taken to increase the role and responsibility of the Central Conferences in the processes of a very large American denomination, but the concerns raised by the 1968 COSMOS report would remain concerns through the next thirty years to the present day. It would be "an American church with overseas outposts" with "lines of authority and communication" running from America to groups overseas. Rather than becoming a "global church," it would continue to be what Janice Love called an "extended-national confessional" church.

CHAPTER FOUR

Today's Challenges to Authentic United Methodist Citizenship

The goal of this book is to make some recommendations about the way we are called to live as a United Methodist Church. To make some sense of the way to proceed, I have tried to portray two things: first, to see who we are as United Methodists; and second, to look briefly at how we got to where we are today. With that information, we can look at the challenges that face us and then review some recommendations. The challenges are formidable, and they have prevented us from making substantial changes for quite a few years. Especially after reviewing the excitement of the discussion and report from the 1968 General Conference, it is curious to review the conferences after that point. The enthusiasm seems to have waned dramatically as seen in the General Conference record, particularly at the 1970 and 1972 General Conferences. Since 1968, the actual changes have been modest; the hope for change, sometimes concretized in petitions, has been large. For this reflection, I skip from 1972 to the late 1980s and then to major, but failed, initiatives in 1996 and 2000.

One way to present the challenge comprehensively is to present the "quandary" facing the UMC. We are stuck between voices emphasizing two needs facing United Methodism: the desire and pressure for autonomy or "self-headedness," and the commitment to an interdependence between the various parts. These pressures are present within the context of a constitutional commitment to Christian unity in the life of the UMC. Hence, this chapter will first define the three desires that put us in the quandary: self-headedness, interdependence, and Christian unity. After reviewing these, we shall look at the mostly unsuccessful attempts of the church leadership to find a way forward and the considerable stumbling blocks that have prevented progress. Case studies at the end of the chapter can make real the discussions so that the conflicting forces can be seen vividly in the life of United Methodist churches. Only then can we turn to what might work in the future.

Before proceeding, I note one important trend. Following 1972, the relationships with the Central Conferences were strengthened within the denomination through many ways, such as greater participation in decision making, membership on the agencies, and greater recognition of the need to create bodies not dominated by the English language. Other changes in the *Book of Discipline* gave the Central Conferences more opportunities to adapt to better meet the ministry and mission needs within different geographical contexts. These changes were partly a reaction to the large number of churches seeking autonomy in 1968–1972. The changes also indicate the growing strength of the Central Conferences and their successful appeal for a system of greater equity and less American domination. This pattern toward greater equity continued in all respects except financial—so much so that today the question of financial exchange and dependence is still the elephant in the room that no one wishes to confront.

There is another important dimension to keep in mind as I articulate these three voices: self-headedness, interdependence, and Christian unity. All three are present *in all contexts* within the American jurisdictions, within Central Conferences, and between affiliated autonomous churches and the UMC.

Voices That Continue to Shape Us

Church has own leaders

The Voice for Self-Headedness

From 1928 on, we have seen the strong passion among many Methodists in younger churches for "self-headedness." The term used throughout the history of the Methodist church was "autonomy." Today there are strong protests against the word "autonomy" by people who very much support the "self-headedness" of younger churches. The word "autonomy" is criticized because a church should never be "autonomous," that is, separated—not connected or not needing other churches across the world. That would go very much against the biblical understanding of the Body of Christ that binds Christians together, which was also a part of the descriptions of United Methodism. Accordingly, from this point forward I will use the term "self-headed." The term comes from the Greek word used commonly in Orthodox church circles, *autocephalous*, which translates literally as "self-headed." Among Orthodox, the term means a church that has its own leadership (in Orthodoxy, often a patriarch) but can be in full relationship and connection with another Orthodox church (sometimes the church from which it emerged). This is what has been meant by "autonomy": a self-governing and self-sustaining church.

We have noted the voices for self-headedness over and over in the accounts listed in the previous chapter. Within the UMC today, we adequately hear the voices of the Central Conference persons. They are among us at General Conference, at the Council of Bishops, and on the agencies. We are less able to hear the voices of persons from those churches that chose to become self-headed. Knowing fully the reasons that led those churches to independence from the predominantly American General Conference is critical for adequate understanding. Here is a list of some reasons that were described in the various reports:

A. National political pressure. Especially for countries in the shadow of a larger and more powerful country, there can be political pressures within a country to separate in all respects from the larger neighbor. This was true in the Methodist Church of Mexico. The Mexican revolution and the strength of nationalism encouraged the Mexican Methodists to seek self-headedness, or the ability to govern without U.S. oversight. Brazil would be another example of a country facing the same pressures.

B. Ecumenical motivation. In some places, divided Methodism was a factor for the creation of a new church that would combine the competing Methodist voices, as seen in Japan, Korea, Burma, and Hong Kong. When countries would have different Methodist voices, there was strong impulse to combine them. For instance, the Korean Methodists wanted to combine two branches of Methodism that were the result of splits in the U.S.: the Methodist Episcopal Church South and the Methodist Protestant Church. The rationality of the unification made the Methodists in these countries ask why it does not occur in other places as well.

C. Greater self-governance. The Central Conferences sometimes desired greater freedom, especially in regard to episcopal supervision (independence of bishops, ability to establish [but not pay] bishops' salaries, episcopal elections, etc.). Today, one of the differences between United Methodist Central Conferences in Africa and the presence of the American-based historic Black Methodist churches in those places lies in the election of bishops. In the historic Black Methodist churches, the last bishop elected at the General Conference is usually sent to Africa for a quadrennium before serving in the United States.[1] The freedom and flexibility of the Central Conferences grew, especially after

1972. This reduced the pressures many of those churches felt to separate from the UMC.

D. *More effective mission.* Mission could be far more effective from independent churches in different parts of the world rather than from a system where all missionaries are sent out from the mother countries. The statistics in mission today are astounding: far greater numbers of missionaries are now sent from developing countries rather than from the traditional mission-sending countries like the United States. This mission philosophy became a major voice that was predominant in both British Methodism and in the Evangelical United Brethren and led those churches to develop a policy of creating independent churches rather than maintaining a Central Conference structure.

E. *Organic union.* The strength of the ecumenical movement caused churches to look enthusiastically at uniting movements within countries and regions of the world (e.g. India, Canada, the Philippines, and Australia). At the heart of the ecumenical movement was the passion for mission. When speaking of the ecumenical movement, I lift up a Baptist missionary. In the 1790s, William Carey, famous in India, called for the churches to work together because their competing missionaries were dividing and impeding the proclamation of Christ. His clarion call of unity in Christ created the vision of the eventual union of churches. The calls for organic union, toward merger of the Church of South India and the Church of North India (even though American Methodists did not join), were strong and proved influential upon the desire for self-governance of the churches.

F. *Political liberation.* Perhaps the strongest voices were influenced by the national and political calls for national independence. The time when many of the churches became independent (in the post–World War II period) coincided with the end of colonialism, the move from colony to independence. The political liberation carried over to the structures of the church.

The Voice for Interdependence and Connection

In one sense, all of the voices call for "interdependence and connection." Who would not since we all understand ourselves to be part of a universal church, part of the Body of Christ? All that was written for United Methodists in those earlier sections that apply to the wider church is, I hope, true for anyone in the Methodist family, for the daughters and sons of John Wesley. But how interdependence and connection are understood can vary. How surprising it is to see such passion in discussions on the global nature of the church. To better understand these voices, I shall first present the voice or "connection" as it is found within the United Methodist structure. The term "connection" traditionally means a closer relationship than the "interdependence" that exists between two self-headed churches (for example, the UMC and the Methodist Church of Brazil). Second, I shall speak of the pressures on United Methodists to not forget that they are part of a broader family that includes other Methodists and Wesleyans, some of whom came out of American Methodism and some who did not.

1. Within the UMC Structure

The Sense of Connection. Throughout its history, the term "connection" has indicated the vital relationships that exist between Methodists. From its earliest times, the term meant the group of people associated with Mr. Wesley. A few years later it was used to describe the relationship between the Methodist societies as well as the relationship to the Church of England of which they were a part. Over the years the term became a broader, organizational principle, and you see references to "the connection," meaning the Methodists in relationship to one another.

Since the term is vital in describing the interdependence among United Methodists, here is the description found in the current *Book of Discipline:*

> Connectionalism in the United Methodist tradition is multi-leveled, global in scope, and local in thrust. Our connectionalism is not merely a linking of one charge conference to another. It is rather a vital web of interactive relationships.
>
> We are connected by sharing a common tradition of faith, including our Doctrinal Standards. (¶ 130)

In another place, the *Discipline* states that "connectionalism is an important part of our identity as United Methodists" and it is experienced in a variety of ways, especially in terms of the mission of the church (¶ 701).

The Council of Bishops, in their 1996 report to General Conference, *A Report on the Global Nature of The United Methodist Church,* placed great emphasis on connectionalism as that which bound the denomination together. Connectionalism, for them, was the way to prevent fragmentation of the church. They said, "We must not allow our essential identity, inclusive fellowship, common mission, distinctive ethos, and visible unity as United Methodists to be broken up into Humpty-Dumpty fragments which cannot be put together again on a global scale" (*Daily Christian Advocate,* p. 170).

The bishops presumed in the document that "autonomy" or self-headedness of churches in various nations meant fragmentation and something less than connection. They feared a danger of fragmentation in the church. They wrote the following to press this vision:

> If [the UMC] does not take this step of becoming a global church, it will most likely face the danger of becoming fragmented into autonomous churches in various nations

of the world, with the American segment becoming merely that—an American fragment of the once future global United Methodist Church! Must we avoid this danger? (*Daily Christian Advocate,* p. 169)

The presumption is clear in the council's report: other relationships, be they ecumenical agreements, unions, covenants, concordats, or any other kind of "connection," are less adequate than a global and structural connection through the UMC structure. The document seems unaware of the judgment placed upon churches that had become self-headed or had become united with other churches in their regions. It also seems insensitive to the vitality and power that can come through Pan-Methodist or ecumenical relationships.

Structural Ways of Building Connection. After the World Methodist Structure Congress in 1970, the UMC put aside its vision for a new Methodist structure based upon the models presented in 1968, and it began a movement lasting until the present to enable the Central Conferences to be more than an appendage to American Methodism. Those changes are interesting:

1. The 1972 conference affirmed their ability to adapt the *Book of Discipline* and instituted judicial procedures in Central Conferences for addressing disciplinary conflicts. Many Central Conferences made changes. The principle that they were able to change the *Book of Discipline* was affirmed by the UMC's Judicial Council as late as 1999 (Council Memorandum No. 859). There are only a couple of restrictions on the breadth of the power of the Central Conferences to make changes. The change cannot be "contrary to the Constitution and the General Rules of the UMC," and it has to keep the "spirit of connectional relationship between the local and general church" (*The Book of Discipline 2000,* ¶ 537.9). I believe that it would surprise many United Methodists to realize that Central Conferences can change/adapt the *Book of Discipline* on nearly all issues, including those that have been the most controversial within the church, such as ministerial orders or sexual conduct.

2. Recent General Conferences have added Central Conference members to the denomination's boards and agencies. Each agency has at least one or two members whose names are put forward by the bishops of the Central Conferences.

3. The 2000 General Conference was in an uproar over the lack of translation for non-English speaking delegates. The 2004 General Conference plans to have written documentation in four languages as well as simultaneous translation on the floor of the conference.

4. A global pension plan is in development. One source of funds for the plan is income from the United Methodist Publishing House that has traditionally been distributed to annual conferences in the United States. The plan faces significant hurdles. Some annual conferences in Africa hardly have any salary for their clergy. It is difficult to build and focus on a pension plan in such circumstances.

5. The Council of Bishops provides opportunities to strengthen relationships with Central Conferences. Primary are the collegial relationships that form in the two weeks per year of interpersonal contact between the bishops (about fifty active bishops from the United States and eighteen from other countries).

The church has created the expectation that Central Conferences need to be present in all groups of the church—from the training of new district superintendents to participation in programs organized by any of the agencies.

How Connection Within the Structure Meets American United Methodist Needs. Another dimension to the "connection" within the denomination involves how it serves the needs of American United Methodists. It is exciting to hear and experience the voices and presence of "family" from far away places like Africa and Asia. When American UMs attend meetings with persons from other parts of the world, the church feels bigger and, somehow, more important to them. The immediacy of the connection is also effective in helping people realize the great economic disparities present among attendees, and gives people opportunity to respond to these obvious material needs. Americans can begin to identify with sisters and brothers in other parts of the world, thus making the world a "global community."

Another positive side to the connection is the gift of the Spirit that comes to people through mutuality of relationships. As people interact in Jesus' name, they find themselves again in God's presence.

However, there are also troubling issues. Why can such a connection only come through people who call themselves United Methodist? Cannot the same interaction happen with Methodists who are in self-headed churches or even with Presbyterians or Lutherans? This raises the same question as raised earlier, "What is it that makes United Methodists so unique that connection only occurs within the family?" I don't think significant distinctives from other Methodists exist.

2. Within the Methodist Family

Even though trends were moving the church to strengthen Central Conferences there was still strong desire across the church for close contact with the many churches that became self-headed. As long ago as 1944, autonomous and united churches sent representatives to General Conference. The process expanded (especially in 1972) and, by 2000, approximately thirty churches sent representatives (with voice but no vote) to General Conference with expenses paid by the UMC (*Book of Discipline 2000*, ¶ 547.3). As I indicated, the term "affiliated autonomy" was developed to indicate the Methodist churches across the world that had emerged from the UMC.[2]

Concordat Churches. In addition to the category of "affiliated autonomous churches," two other relationships have been formed to express the interdependence between the UMC and other members of the Methodist family: First, concordats were considered and established, beginning in

1968. These agreements allow for the exchange of delegates at the highest governing bodies and have been established with three churches: the Methodist Church of Great Britain, the Methodist Church of the Caribbean and the Americas, and the Methodist Church of Mexico. In 1972 the General Conference declared that the Council of Bishops

> shall offer to work out with each affiliated autonomous Methodist or united Church a concordat as provided for in the Constitution and any such concordat recommended by the Council of Bishops shall be presented by it to the General Conference. (*Daily Christian Advocate*, p. 234)

It is unclear to me why the council only pursued concordats with a few churches. For many years there was no other mechanism to form an official relationship with another church. Even though other models exist today, there still is a desire for concordats. As recently as the 2000 General Conference there were petitions for concordats with the Methodist churches in Korea and India. The requests were referred to the Council of Bishops as the place to initiate such actions. And, as we shall see, Puerto Rico and the Council of Bishops are also discussing a possible concordat between the churches.

Act of Covenanting. In 1988, the UMC began to develop a new kind of relationship called an "act of covenanting." The initiative came from agency staff in the General Board of Global Ministries and the General Commission on Christian Unity and Interreligious Concerns (GCCUIC) working with several of the bishops. The vision was to develop an ecclesial relationship church to church. As noted, many churches preferred a relationship that was directly to the UMC rather than mediated through the General Board of Global Ministries. Robert Huston, then GCCUIC general secretary, used language of church relationship found in the Consultation on Church Union to develop a covenant that was ecclesial and focused on topics such as shared mission and witness, exchange of clergy, and

75

recognition of one another's baptism. The *Book of Discipline 2000* uses that language (recognition of one another as authentic churches, eucharistic sharing, recognition of ordained ministries) as well as more general language: to "encourage a new sense of global common cause, mutual support, mutual spiritual growth, common study of Scripture and culture, creative interaction of ministers," and so on (¶ 549).

Ten "acts of covenanting" have been formed and were celebrated at the 1992 or 1996 General Conferences. However, these relationships are not reserved for Methodist churches nor have they become important for the relationship to other Methodist churches. At times, bishops have even paid official visits to covenanting churches without even knowing the covenants were in place. Neither the Council of Bishops, which has oversight responsibility for the covenants, nor the GCCUIC, which should provide assistance, has had the resources to attend the covenants adequately. In regard to both concordats and acts of covenanting, the Council of Bishops indicated in 2001 that it would not establish new relationships until there was clarity about the importance of these relationships for the UMC.

Conference of Methodist Bishops. Another mechanism to express the interdependence between Methodist churches has been the Conference of Methodist Bishops. Historically and theologically, the unity of any church is lodged with the bishops or those who exercise the function of oversight (*episcope*). Therefore, it was logical, when the questions over the relationships with Central Conferences, other Methodist churches, and other parts of the UMC became apparent, that the bishops sought a way to pursue unity.

In 1948, the General Conference established a Conference of Bishops

> composed of all the bishops elected by the General, Jurisdictional and Central Conferences and bishops of the

affiliated autonomous or Methodist (or united) churches, which shall meet in each quadrennium immediately prior to the General Conference or on call of the Council of Bishops. (*Book of Discipline 1948*, ¶ 425)

The expenses for the bishops of other churches to travel to the conference were also paid for by the Episcopal Fund of the UMC. The willingness to provide that support is one long-standing commitment to interdependence.

With all the changes in 1972, one result was the temporary end to the Conference of Methodist Bishops. However, the action was short-lived. In 1980, it was reestablished with support provided for all the UMC bishops and one bishop/chief executive from an affiliated autonomous or united church to attend the conference.

Since that time, there has been considerable confusion, and the conference has not been an effective vehicle for Methodist unity. Since 1988, the language has become more permissive in the *Discipline*. The council calls for the conference when it chooses, and expenses of the non-UMC leaders shall be paid "on the same basis as that of bishops of the UMC" (*The Book of Discipline 2000*, ¶ 428). In my experience, there has been confusion as to the role and purpose of this conference.

First, the confusion in recent years has come from the location and time of the meeting. In 1988 the conference was held in St. Louis immediately before the General Conference. Simultaneously, leaders were invited for the Conference of Methodist Bishops (at UM expense) and non-voting delegates were invited from the same churches to the General Conference (again, at UM expense). Often, at least one of the persons was the same but sometimes not. Leaders who were not delegates were angry that they were not supported financially for the General Conference, and it was awkward.

The next meeting of the Conference of Methodist Bishops was held in Singapore at the World Methodist Council meeting in 1991, but its purposes were not clear and few attended. Additional confusion resulted from holding it at the World Methodist Conference. Were the leaders of the autonomous churches that were not affiliated also invited? Financially, it was difficult as well since the leaders/delegates of affiliated autonomous churches could not be supported by the UMC to both the World Methodist Conference and the General Conference (as restricted in the *Book of Discipline 2000,* ¶ 2403.2).

In 1997, there was a meeting in Seoul, Korea, where leaders of the British Methodist tradition were invited, but they chose not to come. Significant funding for that meeting was provided by the Korean Methodist Church. At present, the council is searching for a more effective way to use this instrument of unity among Methodists.

World Methodist Council (WMC). It would seem that the World Methodist Council would be a powerful instrument of interdependence and connection within the Methodist/Wesleyan family. The organization dates back to the nineteenth century and its membership includes Methodists from the world over. Its strength has been in dialogues with other Christian world communions and the work of some groups closely connected to it, such as the World Federation for Methodist Women and its Evangelism Committee.

However, the council has remained small and largely dominated by The United Methodist Church. Its permanent location in Lake Junaluska, North Carolina, has not helped it to be a strong instrument representing Methodism worldwide. At the same time, the WMC carries so much hope! I noted the decision in 1972 that the WMC be the "adequate instrument for worldwide fellowship and cooperation of all churches of the Methodist traditions" (*Daily Christian Advocate*, p. 239).

In recent years, I have found the council unable to take on the most important issues of inter-relationship and interdependence that face the Methodist community worldwide. For instance, since the early 1990s the UMC, especially its

Board of Global Ministries, has been active in congregational development in Africa. This development has
included countries where Methodist churches already exist.
Autonomous churches in numerous countries were dis-
tressed. The British church also became concerned at the
vigorous evangelism without what was felt to be adequate
consultation and conversation with Methodist partners.
During the 1990s, I wrote on behalf of the United Methodist
Christian unity commission (GCCUIC) asking for the WMC
to facilitate conversations on this topic. I received a letter in
response from the officers indicating that the WMC did not
see this as a role for the organization.

More recently others have pressed the WMC on the same
issue. In 2000 the Council of European Methodists wrote to
the WMC asking them to develop guidelines for
Methodists entering into countries with existing Methodist
churches. That request was followed with a petition to the
2001 World Methodist Council meeting in Brighton,
England, that contained a *Charta Methodistica*. It was
adopted and has been sent to the churches for their review.
It came to the Council of Bishops of the UMC in 2003.

As we shall see, different structural proposals for
Methodism have similarities to the World Methodist
Council. If the WMC had been a stronger organization, the
challenges to United Methodism would have been different. Perhaps United Methodists would not have been so
focused on connection to "family" in other parts of the
world coming solely through a United Methodist structure.

The Voice for Christian Unity

From the beginning of the constitution and throughout
the *Book of Discipline* the commitment to Christian unity has
been at the heart of the Methodist tradition. Its spirit dates
back to famous statements of John Wesley, such as his ser-
mon *The Catholic Spirit*. During the twentieth century the
Methodist churches produced some of the great ecumenical

leaders such as John R. Mott, Charles Parlin, D. T. Niles, Pauline Webb, Philip Potter, and Emilio Castro. The ecumenical voice has been strong in pressing for ecumenical vision and understanding. The UMC (or its predecessors) was a founding member of ecumenical bodies such as the World Council of Churches and various national councils of churches including some in the United States.

One of the strong ecumenical movements of the past was the creation of united churches. Christians in a region or nation would ask why they were divided into denominations. As a consequence many took the great step of "giving up" their particularity of the great tradition of the church for the sake of unity. In such a way churches such as The United Church of Canada and the Uniting Church of Australia were formed. Even the UMC is a result of various mergers from different streams, some which were the result of schism and other streams that merged after years of separate life. Great ecumenical leaders have taught that any church structure is "provisional" in character. That means that it should be willing to die for the sake of the unity of the Body of Christ to which we all are called in many places of Scripture.

However, within the ecumenical movement there has been considerable change. The vision of one large church as an institution has become less appealing. Merger is not now seen as the ideal form of ecumenism. In fact, one highly promoted Plan of Union that came from the Consultation on Church Union (COCU) was defeated at the 1972 General Conference.

Other models for ecumenical relationship replaced the model of organic unity. United Methodists embraced the fellowship found in councils and eventually embraced a vision of reconciliation *within* the diversity of churches throughout the world. For some, these new visions represent a dilution of the ecumenical calling. Others see them as responsive to the Holy Spirit calling Christians in another direction.

Historically, the voice of unity and cooperation was prominent in mission. For example, in the 1916 Panama Congress, when major North American denominational mission agencies were present, the major churches divided Central America into separate mission areas for each church. The Baptists agreed to evangelize Nicaragua, the Episcopalians to concentrate on Panama, and so forth. It happened in the United States as well. When I lived in Vermont, I noticed how the whole state had only eight Presbyterian churches, but when you crossed the border into New York, there was a Presbyterian church in every tiny village. The historical reason was an agreement: the Presbyterians agreed to church planting in New York while the Congregationalists concentrated on missions in Vermont. The "acts of comity" cause me to marvel at the efficiency and be disquieted at the same time.

The interrelationship between the call for evangelism and the desire to have an ecumenical spirit is one obvious place where the voice of Christian unity enters into dialogue with the voices of autonomy and interdependence. Two different illustrations can show the conversation between the voices.

The Fruitful Tension: A Bifocal Vision. Bishop James K. Mathews defined the situation well in 1968. He wrote, "The best current definition of Christian unity speaks of the oneness of all in each place. . . . But the definition goes on to stress unity in relationship also to the church in all other places" (*Daily Christian Advocate*, 1972:245).

He is drawing his language from the famous vision placed before the world at the World Council of Church's Third Assembly in New Delhi in 1961 where the council posed for the world an essential bifocal vision: the Church of Jesus Christ is most fully lived when all the Christians in *one locality* are united together. That means the churches around your town square wherever you may be would be united. At the same time, the church exists across the world and we are interconnected with other members of the church, most visibly seen in our own "family," such as Methodists in Zaire and Methodists in Texas. The Central Conference structure of the UMC has been especially help-ful to us in seeing the upper portion of the bifocal lens—the vision of connection worldwide. The ecumenical voice calls us to look through the lower half of the lens as well—to see the gospel call for unity in our community with Christians close to us in some ways (for example, those in our state or community) yet distant in other ways (Methodists and Pentecostals or Orthodox).

I believe that the voice of connection has been easier to grasp than the voice of Christian unity on many occasions. Ironic as it is, it may be easier for us to feel closer to United Methodists in distant lands than to the Catholics down the street from us. And we may think it easier and more natu-ral to look through the upper, long distance lens rather than to be bifocal.

The Ecumenical Challenge to the "Family." There is a second way the voice of Christian unity enters into tension with our vision of the Methodist "family." What happens when the UMC expands into a country with existing churches that are Methodist or from another tradition? Does our interdependence and unity within the Body of Christ cause us to change our witness and evangelism? I just described the *Charta Methodistica* as a way to address relationships within the family. But the voice of Christian unity calls us to a broader vision of the church. Therefore we would be sen-sitive to churches beyond Methodism that are a part of the Body of Christ. We will see in the description of the church in Russia how difficult this is, especially when the UMC would offer a perspective of the church so different from the one that is prominent in a country.

In the discussion of ecumenical cooperation and mission, another point of view comes from people whose passion for proclamation and evangelism is overflowing. I remember the debate at the World Methodist Council meeting in Brighton over the *Charta Methodistica*. A representative from the Church of the Nazarene asked, "Why do we need any agreements at all? Should not all of us be preaching the gospel every place that we go?" The point is to celebrate each and every place the gospel is proclaimed and *not* to become possessive of a country, people, or community. Recently, I listened to some concerns raised in the United States about the Korean Methodist Church (KMC) forming districts and, possibly, a conference. After hearing some alarmist voices, Bishop David Lawson asked, "Should we not be celebrating and congratulating the KMC for all of their church growth?" The attitude is compelling.

The voice of Christian unity is too often hard to hear. There are deeply committed, ecumenical people who sense a great failure within the ecumenical movement to portray sufficiently the ecumenical mandate as presented in Scripture through passages such as Jesus' prayer that "they may be one" (John 17:11) or in a vision recorded in Ephesians 4:5 of "one Lord, one faith, one baptism." One scholar, Bruce Marshall, believes that God will heap judgment upon us for our complete failure in recent years to achieve greater Christian unity. It seems the will is simply not present in our churches to follow this aspect of the gospel call.[3]

The voices of self-headedness speak for more than just nationalistic reasons to form a church. They can challenge, legitimately, the "voice of Christian unity." For example, some churches hold precious cultural traditions that they fear will be lost through assimilation into a much larger church. For many years, I have attended the discussions of the Commission on Pan-Methodist Cooperation and Union in the United States. The African Methodist Episcopal Church is very reluctant to speak of "union" in the discussion with the United Methodists because the African American tradition that so shapes that church could become diluted if they merged with the much larger United Methodist Church. Even though this does not represent a "global nature" issue, it does reflect some of the aspects of the tensions between self-headedness, interdependence, and Christian unity. That same challenge will face any structural suggestion for a reformation of the UMC.

Responses and Attempts at Structural Change

Throughout the history covered in the previous chapter and in the analysis of the present situation, one theme repeats itself: mere adaptation is not enough; the change in the church has to be thorough and responsive to the tremendous changes in the world. This message has been repeated from the 1932 General Conference to the Council of Bishops meeting in May 2003. And yet, the church has repeatedly opted for minor adaptations while saying that study and change is needed in the future.

We saw how the 1932 conference reflected a need for change such as making the United States a Central Conference, but the Central Conference delegates wanted to continue the status quo. Then in 1968 we also saw the excitement for a World Methodist Structure Conference, but the 1972 General Conference also settled for minimal structural changes.

There is another interpretation: the Central Conferences were able to resist the pressure regularly placed upon them to separate from the mother church. They followed a different model as was noted even seventy-five years ago. Today the same terms of the debate are used. One bishop told me that many Central Conference members are angry at the General Board of Global Ministries for so many years of pressure to become affiliated autonomous churches. I have viewed the GBGM change dramatically since 1992 and have seen it giving far more support, financial and otherwise, to the Central Conferences while they give less to the affiliated autonomous churches. Some groups dispensing UM funds have even restricted the funds so that they could be used only by United Methodists and not by those who separated off from the church.

The reports in the years 1992 through 2000 reflect attempts to create a reformed UM structure. Continuing to underlie them, often unspoken, exists the desire to create a structure that would be welcoming and enticing for the affiliated autonomous churches to "return" to the UMC.

I mentioned in the very beginning of this book the first discussions presented in the Council of Bishops. That material, found in an internal council report in 1990, continued to be worked on and finally found its form in a report to the 1996 General Conference. However, it also fed into 1992 processes.

Connectional Issues Study. The 1992 General Conference called for a Connectional Issues Study (1992 *DCA*, p. 237), which was to be conducted by the General Council on Ministries. It was to "lead the church in a time of discernment, reflection, and study of its mission and its structural needs" and then report with recommendations to the 1996 General Conference. One group with which they were to work collaboratively was the Global Nature of the Church Committee of the Council of Bishops. Their study report in 1996 called for the creation of another study committee, the Connectional Process Team (CPT).

The study called for more study and yet more reflection. It asked for the CPT to consider the recommendations that emerged from the Connectional Issues Study and the Council of Bishops Global Nature report. We look at the recommendations of these two groups and see again the lineage of possible new structures.

The Connectional Issues Study called for regional conferences. The regions would support connections with other conferences (annual and global), elect bishops, perform ministries, handle money, and perform other functions. The Global Conference would "care for all matters of connection for the UMC, specifically, matters of faith, doctrine, polity, purpose, order and vision for the global connection" (1996 *DCA*, p. 250). The terminology popular at that time and repeated throughout the report was that it would be an "interactive organization" with an "interactive process" and an "interactive design." The concept of parallelism was also popular. A "council" structure would be replicated at the local, district, annual conference, regional/global level.

The Council of Bishops' *1996 Report on the Global Nature of The United Methodist Church* called for a Global Council, Global Conference, and Regional Conferences. The Global Conference contains far more structure and responsibility than do any of the previous proposals, including orders of ministry, financial matters, and administrative order. No region could have a majority of delegates. The Global Council would be half bishops and half others. It would coordinate and provide vision, but it would not legislate. And, finally, the Regional Conferences would define their own internal structure. Initially, there would be four regions (North America, Europe, Africa, and Asia/Philippines). Latin America would be further explored, it said.

Four years passed with considerable amounts of money provided for the work of a large Connectional Process Team that met from 1996–2000. It even had representatives from affiliated autonomous churches. So much hope and hard work went into this noble project. At the same time, I do not believe that group ever had significant credibility in the life of the church. And, it seemed to onlookers that the report did not stand a chance to pass at General Conference. The onlookers were right. But the team did offer a vision to the church.

The report to the 2000 General Conference sought to simultaneously address structural issues for local congregations, the annual conferences, and the general church (including global nature questions). The only part of the report accepted contained five "transformational directions":

1. Center on Christian Formation
2. Call Forth Covenant Leadership
3. Empower the Connection for Ministry
4. Strengthen Our Global Connection and Ecumenical Relationships
5. Encourage Doctrinal and Theological Discourse

These and the rest of the report were forwarded to the General Council on Ministries for further study and recommendations to General Conference 2004.

But what was the vision of the Connectional Process Team in terms of the global nature of the church? It was quite similar to the 1932 General Conference's second option. After affirming Central Conference structures they wrote:

> Therefore we recommend that The UMC in the U.S. be structured as a central conference. In doing so, the church in the United States would be reaffirming that it is not the main channel of God's revelation and mercy to those called United Methodists nor is it self-sufficient. (http://gc2000.org/studies/report/3.htm)

The proposed Global Conference would have five hundred delegates, be six days long, with delegates assigned based on membership, beyond two from each annual conference. The report recommended the creation of a Covenant Council (replacing the General Council on Ministries) to make decisions regarding the responsibilities of the Central Conferences in contrast to the Global Conference. The proposal, like the one from the bishops, leaves no place for affiliated autonomous churches. It does say that "we will seek more faithful relationships with these churches and wish to expand mutual dialogue about the future."

Vision. General Conference did take an action called "Living into the Future," which referred both the Global Nature report of the bishops and the Connectional Process Team report to the General Council on Ministries for further work and for recommendations to the 2004 General Conference. At the time of this writing, the recommendations from the GCOM present a model for a new "connectional table" of the general agencies, but they do not address the global nature questions that have pressed upon the church for so many years. That seems tragic!

The Elephant in the Room: Finances and Control of Them

The reports listed above have failed for many complex reasons. One challenge is the question of representation. The reality today is that the United States dominates the General Conference. Much of the rhetoric is to change that fact and create a church that is not dominated by the United States. But, if such a structure is developed, would it be received by those who are accustomed to domination? Would the people who now have the money and decide its expenditure put themselves in a position where they do not have the power to make decisions, even if they are continuing to contribute the vast majority of the funds? I do not think so. One place the issue arises is in the membership of a global conference. Will it be controlled by the United States? Should it be if the United States is home to 75 percent of the United Methodists? Some plans do not allow United States domination (such as the Council of Bishops design). The question is only important if the global conference has control of the finances. If not, then people worry much less about the composition of the conference. The challenge of the finances relates to far more than the composition of the structure of the global church. The challenge also relates to equity, mutual accountability, the sharing of resources, and access to power.

The inequity of finances endangers any structural vision. The UMC has vast differences in wealth and resources between the United States and the two areas where there is the greatest UM growth: Africa and the Philippines. The history and theology of mission is filled with stories about the near impossibility of church development and mission when it is carried out by a financially wealthy part of the church in connection with mission areas of deprivation and poverty. Twentieth century mission history has many examples of developing world churches that have even called for moratoriums of missionaries and aid because of the dependency, paternalism, and even racism that often accompany the transfer of resources. On the other hand, the gospel requires dramatic response to human need. One cannot be faithful, have considerable wealth, be presented with life and death situations requiring support, and not give. So the UMC and its agencies struggle to find appropriate ways to share resources without falling into destructive patterns of giving. The increased decision making or "independence" of the Central Conferences can relieve some of the difficulty. However, I do not think that it has been sufficiently successful.

The Apportionment System. One significant issue facing United Methodism involves the apportionment system. This system provides the mechanism for the UMC membership to support the general work of the church. At the present time, only the annual conferences within the U.S. jurisdictions pay apportionments into the general funds created by the General Conference (with the exception of the General Episcopal Fund).[4] In other words, the funding goes in one direction: from the U.S. to the Central Conferences. In recent years, as the general agencies have increasingly sought to act as agencies for the whole denomination, the practice of only some conferences (that is, those in the U.S.) paying apportionments has become more sensitive. Agencies and General Conference delegates have become aware of the rapidly increasing costs for the denomination: more overseas delegates at conferences and consultations, simultaneous language translation, document translation, increased participation of Central Conference representatives on agencies, and so forth. The list could be far more extensive.

The increasing cost for agencies is also dramatic. For a small agency, one Central Conference delegate from Africa or the Philippines can increase the travel line for board members dramatically. Of course, it would be unjust to exclude that person from participation in many of the smaller committee meetings involved in serving on the agency. The agency I serve, General Commission on Christian Unity and Interreligious Concerns (GCCUIC), will have some meetings that are only one or two days long. Does it make sense to bring a delegate from Mozambique to a meeting for such a short period of time? However, does it make sense not to involve the person in the full life of the commission? For many areas of Central Conference, conference calls prove impossible. The larger boards that have sought to be fully inclusive have had to purchase and use satellite phones that are extremely costly.

Within the GCCUIC, another consideration of Central Conference inclusion arose in discussions of the use of the Interdenominational Cooperation Fund (ICF) to support regional and national councils of churches outside the United States. One European leader argued that, since the European Central Conference does not pay money into this apportioned fund, that fund should not be used to support the non-USA councils. The Europeans find other ways to support those councils. However, some of the African leadership argued that the need was so great that it was appropriate for support to come from the ICF for those councils, especially when United Methodists were often in leadership of them. If such funding is made available across the world, there will be a greater need to have staff outside the U.S. to administer and oversee the funding. It cannot be done adequately from Chicago, Nashville, or New York.

I have wondered why Central Conferences do not pay into the apportionment system. Some suggest that it is too difficult to collect statistics upon which the apportionments are based. Yet, statistics are used for counting delegates to General Conferences! Others have argued that the needs are so great in many areas that it is not appropriate for the Central Conferences to pay. But, one important aspect of the apportionment system is that it is, so to speak, a progressive tax, based on the ability to pay. Many international organizations, such as the World Council of Churches, do expect everyone to contribute based upon one's ability. The principle in that organization is that it is essential for every entity to pay some amount, however little, as a symbol of membership in the larger body. To pay nothing only perpetuates a dependency pattern that is dangerous to the health of the church.

Salaries for Bishops. One glimpse of actual numbers might be helpful. Approximately 30 percent of the Episcopal Fund goes to support the Central Conference bishops. Additional costs for relocation of bishops caught up in wars, the destruction or loss of equipment and housing, and additional costs for medical care in the United States (and cost of supplementary episcopal supervision) are not considered in the number here that addresses only regularly anticipated costs.

One can list many other difficulties raised by financial issues—usually not faced by the denomination. Here is an example that has been apparent to me as I work in ecumenical circles but is not visible within the denomination. Consider the salary of a United Methodist bishop in an area of the world of enormous poverty such as Central Africa. The compensation is nearly equivalent to a bishop from the United States but the cost of living differential is huge. First, with that larger salary, that bishop is far wealthier than the bishop of another church in the same area. Must that not affect the relationship between those two church leaders? In ecumenical circles, stories are told of the anger that it produces, plus the accusations of the way the UM bishop is beholden to the American church (and, in that case, it is seen as an American church). Second, the salary of the bishop is also far greater than the salaries of the UM clergy that serve under his leadership (all African bishops are men). In fact, some clergy have tiny salaries, hardly enough to live on. I believe that, like in the United States, the salaries of the bishops in any country should be based upon the average of the salaries of those persons who serve under their leadership. Any reader can imagine that the relationship between the bishop and the clergy must be affected by a huge disparity of income. Furthermore, one can imagine the pressure it places on the election of bishops! The plan for a global pension plan must also be challenged by financial inequities such as this one.

Resources for Central Conferences. At present, resources are made available to the Central Conferences in many different ways. Increasingly, agencies are offering programs and resources, encouraged by the increasing number of Central Conference representatives who serve on those agencies. Additionally, Central Conference bishops and representatives itinerate through the U.S. annual conferences and assist in the establishment of partner relationships between the U.S. churches and Central Conference churches. The UMC has only begun to assess the extent of this kind of support for the Central Conferences. The increasing support received by the Central Conferences is very attractive to affiliated autonomous churches as well. Many of those churches (who are struggling for survival) had become autonomous out of spiritual conviction. Now they see the great appeal of better access to resources through the UM structures and wonder if being a Central Conference is the only avenue of access to those resources.[5]

Case Studies: How Do These Challenges Look in Real Life?

I have tried to describe the reasons it has been so difficult to find a new structure for The United Methodist Church. However, it may be far easier to understand the issues I have outlined when seen more concretely. Here are some examples of ways in which Central Conferences have faced the calling to spread the gospel and have responded to the three voices of self-headedness, connection, and Christian unity at the same time. All of the places have dramatically different stories to tell.

The Philippines

For many years, there has been a divide within the Philippine Central Conference and its annual conferences between persons who wish to see the United Methodists in the Philippines as autonomous of the United States, and those who wish to maintain the "connection" as part of the structure of the UMC. Historically, the search for authentic unity in the Philippines precedes the union of the UMC in 1968. In 1948, the Evangelical United Brethren joined the Disciples of Christ, Presbyterians, Congregationalists, and some Methodists to form The United Church of the Philippines, while many from the American Methodist tradition did not. (As a result of this merger, both The United Church and the UMC in the Philippines are separate members of the World Methodist Council.) Within the United Methodist Philippine body, there have been many years of voting over the question of autonomy. At times, those votes have seemed successful only to be mired in political quagmires, often presided over by bishops coming from the United States. On numerous occasions, the struggle between the different groups has overflowed into discussions in the Council of Bishops, the General Conference, and in other forums of the UMC. Usually, the U.S. participants observing the debate have little understanding of the depth and complexity of the discussion.

In recent years, the debate has made it difficult for bishops to be elected in the Philippines. Since a vote of two-thirds is needed for election and the church was evenly divided, and since the question of autonomy was paramount, the elections were arduous. At times, retired bishops served extra terms as a result of the impossibility of the election. During the last few years, new bishops have been elected who support autonomy.

The growth of the church in the Philippines, and the unchanging rules of *The Book of Discipline,* have made it very difficult for the United Methodists in the Philippines to appeal to General Conference for autonomy. Presently, there are nineteen annual conferences in the Philippines. In order for an appeal to General Conference to go forward, *all* the annual conferences must approve petitions for autonomy. Therefore, if eighteen conferences wish autonomy and one opposes it, the status quo continues.

The present situation becomes more difficult because of the way in which classic concepts of the Wesleyan tradition are at stake. Bishop Emerito Nacpil has written forcefully that the autonomy movement is a violation of connectionalism. In a certain way, structural separation in favor of autonomy does involve a certain "distancing" from other United Methodists, especially since the UMC has moved in recent years to strengthen Central Conference relationships and to distance the affiliated autonomous churches. However, connectionalism cannot mean only "connection" between people called United Methodist in different parts of the world. It is also related to catholicity, universality, and *oikoumene* (the "household of God"), terms that portray a "connection" not bound by denominational lines.

The situation of U.S. United Methodists is also difficult in this deliberation process. Without significant contact with Philippine United Methodists, it is difficult to understand the yearning for self-headedness among them and the reasons structural separation from the large U.S. United Methodist community might be positive and needed for the mission and ministry of the churches in the Philippines. The primary question need not be, "What preserves or strengthens the UMC?" Rather, a prior question asks how the mission and ministry of the church of Jesus Christ is best accomplished for discipleship, while living out the distinctives and gifts of the Wesleyan tradition.

Africa

The context of Africa poses the most difficult questions for the UMC with regard to relationships and structure. I articulated some of the issues earlier in this chapter. In so many places, the needs are so large that there is little time for reflection. The church's goal needs to be to find ways to share resources immediately in order to save more people from suffering, whether they be in Angola, Zaire, Zimbabwe, or South Africa. The United Methodist News Service provides one compelling story after another of the need, and of the success of links that have formed between United Methodists in the United States and congregations and annual conferences in Africa. Bishops of the Central Conferences have also itinerated through annual conferences, sharing the story of the growth of the faith and of United Methodism, as well as the needs within their conferences. The agencies of the church and the Council of Bishops are searching for ways to give more priority to work in Africa. As directors go to visit Africa, the need for resources is paramount and other issues become secondary. No matter how the structure of the UMC changes, large or little, the need for involvement and assistance in Africa shall be paramount.

While trying to respond to the need, we can also seek to live more closely to a vision of a sustainable United Methodist Church structure. We do not have one now! Of course, the situation requires deep understanding. Daunting issues in Africa include protracted military conflict, the inadequacy of colonially established national boundaries not compatible with tribal boundaries, deprivation caused by natural disaster and disease, difficulties of technological transfer, and so on.

In addition to these questions there also needs to be consideration of the relationships within the Wesleyan/ Methodist family. For historical and political reasons, Africa contains many places where there are now numerous Methodist churches with sensitive relationships between them. The issue of protocol and the need for a "Methodist charter" of relationship emerges from some of the sensitive overlap between Methodist groups. Outlining briefly some of these situations may help to clarify the situation that exists.

1. Kenya. This nation, as a former British colony, has had a well-established Methodist Church. In recent years, however, because of political reasons, The United Methodist Church has had a bishop residing in Kenya. Around that bishop's presence and community, United Methodists have been engaged in ministry. In recent years, numerous discussions have taken place about what is appropriate hospitality among Methodists, whether congregational development should occur in regions where another Methodist church resides, and how the situation is affected when the United Methodists present have access to considerable amounts of resources that are not available to other Methodist communities. Some of these questions, especially financial ones, are present in other places in Africa and raise issues that are difficult to discuss. The UMC in Kenya and the Methodist Church in Kenya have sought through dialogue to resolve some of these questions. More recently, the development of the Kenya Methodist University with considerable support from United Methodists in the U.S. has led to new tensions. Africa University in Zimbabwe is a long-standing commitment of the UMC, which is not receiving the support it needs from some jurisdictions in the United States. Does the solicitation for Kenya Methodist University hurt that fund-raising? Some United Methodist leaders associated with Africa University assert that there has been an intentional confusion between the two projects in order to raise more money for the Kenya Methodist University.

2. South Africa. Again, South Africa has had a strong Methodist church that has come from British roots, The Methodist Church of Southern Africa. In recent years, United Methodist communities have begun meeting in South Africa and have expressed interest in formalizing their relationships, becoming affiliated with the UMC through annual conferences that are present in nearby nations, or forming their own annual conferences.[6] Some of the communities have formed because of the movement of peoples from one country to another (thus taking their affiliations with them). Other communities have formed for other reasons, sometimes for the benefits of affiliation with a large, international church. Then, in other cases, congregations have desired affiliation when they have broken off from the pre-existing Methodist church in the area. And, finally, the situation also includes other Methodist bodies from other Methodist traditions.[7]

Several issues have become apparent in the South Africa circumstance. First, decisions regarding the creation of new areas and congregations are made within the Central Conferences themselves. At the same time, when tensions arise, they are taken to ecumenical leadership of the denomination who are present in international arenas, such as the Ecumenical Officer of the Council of Bishops or the General Secretary of the General Commission on Christian Unity and Interreligious Concerns. Most often, the ecumenical leaders have little knowledge of the developments and decisions that led to the tensions. Better patterns need to develop to address such situations.

Second, there are few opportunities for the Methodist leaders in Africa to be in communication with one another. Thankfully, new meetings have developed in Africa among the leadership to which the UM bishops and representatives have been able to go.

Third, when the UMC Central Conferences do make decisions about new congregational development or other missional needs, there is no common source of information or understanding since there is no common *Book of Discipline,* and the only part of that book which is required for all United Methodists is the Constitution.[8] The "Methodist Charter" being developed in the World Methodist Council would be an ecumenical document that could be supplemented by denominational understandings. The World Methodist Council is not able presently to meet these communication and resource needs for the UMC.

3. Ivory Coast. In a fascinating recent development, the Methodist Church of the Ivory Coast has requested to join The United Methodist Church. Considering that it is a church with approximately one million members, the possible action raises interesting questions for the UMC. The roots of that church go back to the nineteenth century. From the early 1920s, the church has been affiliated with British Methodism and was part of the districts of that church until it became autonomous in 1963. Many of their reasons for joining the UMC may involve the benefits that would come from the connection to the larger, international church.

What influence its membership might have when it joins the UMC is not clear. Also, the process is unclear by which they would join the UMC and what kind of consideration would take place in the Commission on Central Conference Affairs at General Conference. The opportunity is great for the growth of the UMC through this new addition. However, it does raise questions about the doctrinal coherence of United Methodism, the process for churches to join, and the need for some forum to assess the impact of the decision upon the rest of the denomination. Finally, a key question should involve the way that the change would affect the mission and ministry of the church of Jesus Christ in the Ivory Coast and in other parts of the world.

4. General Comments on the Church in Africa. United Methodism has offered wonderful opportunities for United Methodists within the U.S. to experience the "global church," that is, a chance to see how Christianity is practiced in a society dramatically different from their own. United Methodists from the U.S. also realize how much they have to learn from African church people. There is a vitality and enthusiasm to the faith often missing in the U.S. churches. Cannot some "mutuality in mission" be beneficial to the UMC? But how important is the denominational membership for that connection to be present? Can the structural relationship of an African church with a U.S. church be detrimental in any way to its mission and ministry? Does the present structure of the UMC make relationships possible that are equitable and just? Historically, the mission movement has been greatly concerned by the way in which cultural and financial differences have hurt the work of mission because of the creation of dependencies, paternalism, and even the impact of an institutional racism. Finally, can the catholicity and the unity of the church work across denominational lines so that the same kind of benefits can come from international and intercultural contact between churches that are not structurally related? The constitutional commitments of the UMC to the unity of the church obligate that these questions be asked within the discussions of global nature and the UMC.

Russia

The UMC's presence in Russia began during the winter of 1990 when the United Methodist Committee on Relief was assigned to be a "lead agency" in offering assistance to the people of Russia during a difficult winter.[9] Following the work there, a program of congregational development began and procedures were put in place in 1992 to provide leadership through the placement of a bishop in Moscow and the beginning of a process for the development of an annual conference.

The Russian Orthodox Church became angry at the placement of a bishop in Moscow. They asked the following question: Given the fact that we have been in close conversation and in membership together in the World Council of Churches for nearly forty years, how is it that you can open churches in Russia and place a bishop in Moscow without any consultation with us? Indeed, it is a valid question. Does our mutual accountability to each other through the ecumenical movement mean nothing? At the same time, many realized there was a different ecclesial issue behind their anger: they considered Russia as Orthodox, canonical territory. United Methodists are not welcome to convert the Orthodox. (This is said even when only a small fraction of the Orthodox attend church. The Russian Orthodox Church considers all Russians Orthodox.)

United Methodist ecumenical leadership traveled several times to Russia to meet with Russian Orthodox leaders. The rift is not healed, and the Russian Orthodox have persistently criticized United Methodists in ecumenical circles, accusing them of proselytism. One important point has not been easily discussed: the UMC does offer a theological vision to the Russian people that is very different from what the Russian Orthodox Church offers them. A big difference is the opportunity for laypeople to become pastors and leaders of the church. Another contrast could be the intense study of scriptures in United Methodism. Other differences could lift up the Wesleyan distinctives that would lend support to the global nature, at least of Methodism.

One other factor is present in the Russian situation that is important and prevalent in Europe. The tiny churches that are often part of the UMC in this continent gain legitimacy and support from their connection with the UMC in its "global nature." The UMC community in Russia has access that it would not have otherwise to strong ecumenical witness and support. Another example of support for a small church would be in Norway. In the face of the predominant Church of Norway (Lutheran), the Norway UMC is better able to be in dialogue with the Church of Norway because it is part of the larger church. The UMC in Norway is seen differently, and the members of the church enter into dialogue with the predominant (national) church on different grounds because they are part of the larger UMC. This was especially apparent when the treaty was signed between the Church of Norway and the UMC of Norway.

Puerto Rico

For many years, the Methodist churches of Puerto Rico were part of The United Methodist Church. (The Evangelical United Brethren churches became part of the United Church of Puerto Rico.) They were part of an Episcopal Area in the Northeast Jurisdiction. However, there was a strong desire by Puerto Ricans for many reasons to form an autonomous church as had most of their Central and Latin American Methodist neighbors. Therefore, they petitioned the General Conference and, in 1992, were granted the status of an affiliated autonomous church.

Yet, in many ways the situation of Puerto Rico is unique. This was the first time that United Methodists within a U.S. territory had sought autonomy. Puerto Rican United Methodists had never been part of the Central Conference structure. In the negotiations at General Conference, there was agreement on a transitional plan for eight years that involved the continued financial support of the Methodist Church in Puerto Rico, the continued participation of Puerto Ricans in boards and agencies of the UMC, presence and participation of the Puerto Rican bishop in the UMC's Council of Bishops, continued participation in the UMC Pension Plan, and a variety of other forms of connection. That agreement was scheduled to end in 2000, but it was extended for four years. Presently, there is a proposal within the Council of Bishops that continues a strong, unique relationship with the UMC. At first, the desire was to articulate a "covenant" with Puerto Rico since they had established an "act of covenanting" in 1992 (in addition to the petition that granted the special relationship). However, after discussions at the Council of Bishops in April 2003, the proposal is to establish a concordat with Puerto Rico that might someday give them the right to vote at General Conference.[10] The proposals will go from the Council of Bishops to the 2004 General Conference. Of course, if Puerto Rico establishes a concordat, other churches might wish to do so as well.

The Puerto Rican situation is important since it seeks a more significant place at the table than has been possible before for an affiliated autonomous church. Within the context of the changes since the 1972 General Conference that have weakened the relationships with affiliated autonomous churches and strengthened the relationships with Central Conferences, the proposed relationship poses some middle ground for new connection. Puerto Rico has a unique relationship for several reasons: its presence on U.S. territory, its emergence from a jurisdiction and not from a

Central Conference, and its serving a vital role in providing resources and expertise in Hispanic ministry within the five U.S. jurisdictions of United Methodism. Apart from these considerations, is this a model for a middle ground between being in the Central Conference and complete separation? Could this model be used by other churches? How would the strengthened relationship relate to the present categories of concordat and act of covenant? The Puerto Rico situation will be closely followed by other churches who want a stronger relationship than is presently possible for autonomous churches but who also want to be self-headed.

CHAPTER FIVE

United Methodist Citizenship: A Search for Institutional Faithfulness

Shall We Become a Global Church? Many reports have assumed that the UMC must be a "global church" to be faithful to its call and to its origins in John Wesley's vision that "the world is our parish." In the 1996 Council of Bishops *Report on the Global Nature of The United Methodist Church*, the bishops describe the "Elements of a Global Vision":

> The *self-understanding* of The United Methodist Church is that it is a church and is part of the universal church (¶ 4, Article IV of the Constitution of The United Methodist Church, *The Book of Discipline* 1992). If so, then it bears the essential marks of the church, which are unity, holiness, catholicity, and apostolicity. These essential features of the church must be expressed both locally and globally (1996 General Conference *Daily Christian Advocate,* vol. 1, p. 169).

As I have argued as well, we are part of the universal church, and it is absolutely right that we should bear the "marks of the church" as stated in the Nicene Creed: "We believe in one holy catholic and apostolic church." And, yes, it is true that the marks of the church need to be expressed locally and globally. But does that make it a requirement for The United Methodist Church to have an international structure in order to be an authentic church? Is the Evangelical Lutheran Church in America less a church than the UMC because it does not have a structure geared for membership in other countries? Of course not! Many churches in the world (perhaps with the exception of the Roman Catholic Church) are fully "church" because they are *part* of the universal church and do not expect their own denominational structures to be the universal church. There are other churches that affirm they are the "universal church" and everyone else is outside the church. But our Constitution does not permit such an exclusive self-perception. Our bishops should not affirm that our denomination needs to be the whole church either.

In the next paragraph, the bishops' report says that we are aimed at "inclusiveness" and that "This inclusiveness cannot be local only; it is also global." Again, the report confuses the UMC with the church of Jesus Christ. I described this dangerous confusion in the section "Are We a Self-satisfied Church?" Our structure need not be international to be "fully church." But that also does not mean that it shouldn't be international.

What a gift the "global UMC church" can be! Recently, I attended the Troy Annual Conference and watched and marveled at the presence and involvement of United Methodists from the Mozambique Annual Conference. Troy Conference members (from New York State and Vermont) had been to Mozambique and here was a team of a dozen people from Africa bringing their gifts and friendship to Vermont. The offerings were taken and money was collected to help with projects in Mozambique that were described and made vivid to the members of Troy Conference. There is even a firm in Vermont that makes land-mine removal equipment whose owner was a United Methodist. Maybe something could be worked out to meet urgent needs in Mozambique in regard to land mines! Nothing can match the personal connection to reinforce the nature of unity found in the Body of Christ.

Connections like those at Troy Conference (that are repeated many times in annual conferences throughout the United States) do not depend on everyone being United Methodist. Church World Service, the World Council of

Churches, the World Methodist Council, or World Vision could help with similar kinds of projects. Nevertheless, there is something exciting about it "being in the family."

As I have noted, the dangers of this vision are less apparent. However, they are ever present, especially when the "family" type of connection becomes the normal method. In mission history, ecumenical organizations have often developed precisely because of these dangers: missing the places of greatest need because they are less visible to the giving church's eyes, dependency structures that develop, having the giving dependent upon the abilities of the individuals who get to travel to the wealthy country, and the issues that surround such privileges.

How Do Other Global Churches or Church Families Organize?

Before I propose changes in the United Methodist structure, it might be helpful to look at the models used by other church families who are organized internationally. First, I indicated earlier that the Roman Catholic Church is the only truly "global" church including some 20 percent of the world's population and extending into nearly every country of the world. Next, we can learn from the Anglican communion, partly because it is close theologically to the UMC. And, finally, there are the Orthodox, the Lutherans, the free churches, and others.

Roman Catholics. The Roman Catholic Church, out of which we came as Methodists and Protestants, maintains its unity through a strong theological understanding of the bishop. A "local church" is the part of the church that is under the authority of a bishop. Roman Catholics do not use the term "local church" like we do to refer to a particular parish or congregation. When talking globally, the Roman Catholics would refer to all the Catholics in the United States as the U.S. local church! Or the Catholics within a diocese with numerous parishes would be a "local" church. They are "local" in contrast to the universal church that is based in Rome under the authority of the Pope who is the Bishop of Rome. This foundational understanding of the bishop, and then that bishop's relationship to other bishops and especially to the Bishop of Rome (the Pope), creates a cohesive and functional structure for the Roman Catholic Church. In learning about Catholicism, it is so important to recognize the importance of the bishops to comprehend how the Roman Catholic Church functions.

Of course, this structure is also full of challenges. Since the nineteenth century, the role of the Bishop of Rome has been elevated to "infallibility," so that, under particular circumstances, he cannot be wrong. In more recent years, many Catholic theologians have sought to restore the dimension of collegiality among the bishops and grant more authority to all the bishops when gathered together in council.

As you compare this system to United Methodism, note the importance of the Pope for holding the church together and providing for its unity. Our difficulty is to find a way to embody unity among the parts of Methodism without creating a similar structure that would be so much against our more democratic and lay-empowering structure. The General Conference would need to enable the kind of identity and unity that the Pope provides in the Catholic Church.

Orthodox. I have mentioned some of the difficulties the present UM structure poses to ecumenical organizations. Not many large Protestant denominations have membership in more than one country. The World Methodist Council, for instance, counts UMs outside the United States as belonging to other churches (such as The United Methodist Church of Zimbabwe). The World Council of Churches considers the U.S. United Methodists the "mother church" with the other UM communities across the world as extensions of the mother church. The WCC thinks in that way because that is how it treats the Orthodox.

Structurally, the UM/Orthodox comparison is helpful. Janice Love had categorized the UMC as an "extended-national confessional" church like some Orthodox churches (those that are not truly global). However, there is a huge difference between Orthodoxy and United Methodism. Like the Catholics, the Orthodox churches have a locus of authority in one person, the patriarch (or pope). I do not believe that the General Conference provides the cohesion and unity that comes through obedience to the patriarch. The patriarch is intimately connected to the bishops, who are connected to the dioceses and parishes across the world. The UMC does not match that degree of hierarchy, nor would it want to. Like the Catholics, there is less lay leadership in Orthodoxy.

Anglican. Here we turn to a tradition much closer to our own. Methodism emerged from the Church of England and is close to it theologically. Our Articles of Religion were copied almost literally from those of the Church of England. At the same time, we have separated structurally and separated in how we understand the church, especially in the Methodism that emerged in America.

The whole history is not critical to relate here. But it is important to remember that Methodism adopted democratic and representative practices and principles beginning with and following the Christmas Conference in Baltimore in 1784 when Francis Asbury was elected bishop. The Anglican tradition followed the principle mentioned earlier of encouraging self-headedness of its mission churches as they became established. So the Episcopal Church, USA, and the Church of England have few members in other countries. At the same time, however, they have found remarkable ways to maintain "connection" more strongly than many other traditions (such as the Lutheran and Reformed).

What are these forms of Anglican connection? First, there is the remnant of a patriarch in the Archbishop of

Canterbury. Although he has no legislative or juridical authority, he does serve as a center for unity. Through that office, the provinces (that is, the self-headed national churches) are held in a symbolic unity with one another. Furthermore, the Archbishop convenes all the bishops of Anglicanism once every ten years at Lambeth, England. Here again is an intentional way to link the churches one with another into a unified whole. Other less significant structures serve the unity as well: a Consultative Council that meets regularly and a regular meeting of the primates (the head bishop of each of the provinces). Can we learn from any of these unifying structures?

Other Churches. The Lutherans are organized entirely along national lines—not surprising, since most Lutheran churches were first organized as state churches. They do have a strong confessional organization, The Lutheran World Federation, connecting them together. Reformed and Baptist churches are loosely connected. One can expect that because of their "free church" tradition that focuses upon the role and autonomy of the local congregation. More interesting to us, perhaps, are some Pentecostal churches. For instance, the Assemblies of God moved away from an extended-national model to make national churches self-headed. The superintendents of each of the national churches attend a General Council that has consultative but not legislative functions. There is also a World Assemblies of God Fellowship that meets every few years to consult and discuss mutual concerns.

By looking at these different arrangements we get a glimpse of how different churches seek to be connected and interrelated—some families far more interdependent than others. Of course, the detailing of the different families leaves out countless churches that are not connected to other churches, inside or outside of their country. In fact, the emergence of large, independent congregations is visible in nearly all parts of the world—from Willow Creek,

USA, to Zaire. Often those churches focus upon a charismatic person and then face crises of transition when the person retires or dies. But the churches that are parts of larger traditions or families can signal to us important patterns of connection.

Principles for Institutional Faithfulness and Change

With these illustrations, I turn to what may be principles for faithfulness for The United Methodist Church. How do we sense that the church will best serve the coming of the Reign of God? How will we best serve the church's mission to "make disciples for Jesus Christ"? How will we best act like the disciples upon whom Jesus poured out his breath and said, "Receive the Holy Spirit" (John 20:22)?

I have described how previous attempts to change the structure have failed. Since 1928, when the Central Conferences were created, there have only been modifications of the structures despite urgent calls for transformation. I suggest that we consider change, initially, in two phases. The first phase would create a UMC structure that preserves that connection that people believe is so important and, at the same time, would provide opportunity for "self-headedness" to United Methodists in different regions of the world. The result would be a denominational structure ready to move into a new connection, locally and globally, with other United Methodists. A second phase would seek to assist in the unity among Wesleyans and Methodists across the world. Changes such as these are needed for us if we truly seek to live out Jesus' prayer for the oneness of the church of Jesus Christ. Continuing the status quo is contrary to the Bible!

Here are principles that could govern all changes. In all our changes we shall:

1. Uphold the rich tradition and faithful discipleship of the UMC.
2. Envision a structure that recognizes and strengthens the interdependence between United Methodists and other Methodists throughout the world.
3. Remember the Constitutional foundation of the UMC as a part of the universal church of Jesus Christ, which we understand, theologically, to be the Body of Christ.
4. Understand that any institutional structure, even the UMC, is a provisional and temporary structure hoping to find the unity of the one church to which Jesus Christ and the Holy Scriptures call us.
5. Commit ourselves to ask at all times whether the changes we propose enhance or diminish the opportunity to proclaim the mission and ministry of Jesus Christ in each place.
6. Keep the three voices of self-headedness, interdependence, and Christian unity in mind and heart as we proceed.
7. Work toward a church that expresses the oneness of all in each place and a unity in relationship to the church in all other places.

A Possible Structure

With such a tradition of failure to change within United Methodism, it seems foolish for me to suggest particular, structural changes for the UMC. However, I do believe that a new model is necessary and want to offer a suggestion as to changes over time that can enable the UMC to be a stronger church, positioned for new missions and ministries and faithful to its traditions. The challenge is to create a structure that is faithful to the three voices (or desires) that beckon us. To accomplish this, the self-headedness voice needs to be evident in regional areas far more than reflected in today's structure.

Let me illustrate how unclear it is today. The UM churches in Europe have a need for connection with other United Methodists that is very different from the needs in Africa. In Europe, the United Methodist community is tiny. Many Methodists believe they could be quickly swallowed within the hugeness of Lutheranism (in areas such as Scandinavia and Germany). Ecumenical agreements can hold that danger! One church, the UMC of Norway, has formed a treaty with the country of Norway that establishes a formal relationship with the state church, The Church of Norway (Lutheran). The recognition of the size of the UMC in the United States helped in the development of that agreement. However, that agreement seems not to involve United Methodists outside of Norway. How can that be under our present structure? The reason is that self-headedness in fact already exists in that Central Conference. Other financial examples of self-headedness are given in this book. On the other hand, in Africa, the desperate need is for the sharing of resources. Financially, there exists an enormous dependency while at the same time other spiritual gifts to offer to United Methodists in the United States.

Therefore, I propose a structure in phase one that maintains the connection and ensures self-headedness on a regional level. How much self-headedness is given to annual conferences is a decision that the regions would make for themselves.

Phase One

General Conference should establish a task force to reconstitute the UMC *with its present members* so that its global structure is based on the Principles for Institutional Faithfulness. The goal shall be a UMC that continues to have members in different parts of the world. Yet, the new structure shall enable greater self-headedness in the regions for the sake of their mission and ministry. Here are the different parts of a new structure:

General Conference

There would be a General Conference to provide a common basis for ministry, membership, and episcopacy. The conference would have representation from regions based upon their annual conferences. The General Conference would be preceded by a meeting of the bishops of all the regions who would report to the General Conference.

A common constitution including the basic, theological tenets/distinctives of Methodism would be affirmed by all regions. Sufficient agreement would be present to ensure exchange of mission and ministry, shared Eucharistic fellowship, and other such items presently existing in the Act of Covenanting described in *The Book of Discipline 2000* (¶ 549) and in the *2000 Book of Resolutions*.

The mutual accountability of all United Methodists to one another would be encouraged theologically, socially, and financially. There would need to be recognition of the great disparities between regions that could lead to the connectional sharing of resources.

A further connectional structure for the UMC may be developed by the regions (see below).

Regional Conferences

These conferences could be similar to Central Conferences today and would serve as the prime instrument of governance in relationship to The United Methodist Church as a whole. The following would apply to them:

They would be composed of churches located in different nations or portions of nations. There may be several regions in one continent, such as the Central Conferences in Africa today.

Regional Conferences of the UMC would be self-governing and self-sustaining in their ministerial and administrative structure.

The Regional Conference itself would determine the degree of self-headedness accorded to the annual conferences or subregional groupings. For instance, the five U.S. jurisdictions may prefer to be separate regions or they may wish to be one region with various levels of self-headedness in the subregions (jurisdictions).

All regions would be required to contribute to the support of the UMC and its General Conference based on their ability to contribute financially. The UMC may have some staff that serve all regions. Or it may choose to have a consultative council to nurture the connection across the church. This consultative council could be a Council of Presidents of the regions or subregions, many of whom may be bishops. Costs for this structure could be shared among the regions.

Participation in ecumenical organizations would be regional or subregional.

Representation would not be developed in such a way to reward small Methodist regions in General Conference participation.

Each region would have its own *Book of Discipline*. A constitution and other Wesleyan distinctives would be common to all the regions and sufficient for shared fellowship and ministry between the regions.

Other Structures of Connection

As we learned from looking at other church models, there could be other important channels to uphold and strengthen the connection. I have already mentioned the General Conference, the Council of Bishops, and a consultative council. Additionally, there could be all sorts of exchanges, covenants between annual conferences, ministerial exchanges, lay institutes, interrelated service projects, and many other possible programs. The connection can remain as vital as the people of the church desire it to be under this proposed structure.

Phase Two

The United Methodist Church anticipates and hopes for a greater structural as well as ecclesial relationship with other Methodist churches, especially those that emerged from the American Methodist tradition. Phase one would provide a polity and structure that includes self-headedness in regions and prepares the church for new and renewed relationships with other Methodist churches. This would be done in the context of interdependence/connection and a recognition of the larger, ecumenical church. Phase two would be limited to churches of the Methodist tradition with the hope that some day another phase could anticipate greater unity within the Church of Jesus Christ. But we need to move step-by-step. Phase two would implement mechanisms to provide for the welcome of other Methodist communities into the region as self-headed churches equal to those that have evolved in phase one. In phase two additional regions may be added to the global United Methodist Church since the Methodists who join would not emerge from the pre-phase one UMC.

Methodists in affiliated autonomous churches continue to express deep desire to be in closer relationship with United Methodists. We know that they are unable to join the UMC in its present structure. At the April 2003 Council of Bishops meeting, during the conversations about Puerto Rico, Bishop Juan Vera of the Methodist Church of Puerto Rico was asked why Puerto Rico would not become a Central Conference if they wanted a closer relationship. It was obvious from his response that the Puerto Ricans would not consider such an option. Neither would many affiliated autonomous churches, such as the churches of Latin America. But, I believe that, after phase one took place, then Latin American Methodists would be very interested in joining a structure based upon self-headedness *and* interdependence. So would others across the world. Phase two could begin as soon as phase one was implemented and functioning. In fact, phase one is necessary in order for phase two to someday happen.

I hoped at first that I could envision the two phases occurring at once. Many of the structures of previous years have sought to create a proposal that could include affiliated autonomous churches immediately. I do not believe that it is possible. Only when United Methodists find a structure that combines self-headedness and interdependence will Methodists across the world find a denomination that they would wish to join.

Conclusion

In 1968, Bishop Barbieri, from the Buenos Aires area of the Latin America Central Conference, said the following to the General Conference:

> At the summit, therefore, we would have a world conference through which we would seek interdependence, so that all the churches therein involved could learn from each other on an equal basis and receive such mutual assistance and inspiration as necessary, up to the day when we shall belong to a larger fellowship in pursuit of the final aim of coming to be one flock under the leadership of the One Pastor. (*1968 General Conference Journal*, p. 243)

His words hint at the step-by-step process which we undergo in seeking to be faithful to the call of the Holy Spirit and the commandments of the Bible. The final call is one of Christian unity. Of course, this vision tells of what we have been given as well, what we can do in the present age. For those who have ears to hear, it gives us a glimpse of the Reign of God to which we are called.

We hope that God is calling The United Methodist Church into the twenty-first century in new and profound ways. May our hope lead to action and commitment. As people called Methodist, may we seek, as John Wesley said, to "spread scriptural holiness across the land (world)."

Notes

Chapter One

1. See *Called to Be Neighbors and Witnesses,* adopted by the General Conference 2000 and available from the General Commission on Christian Unity and Interreligious Concerns.

Chapter Two

1. Love, pp. 100-102. *Is Methodism a World Church?* Found in *The Ecumenical Implications of the Discussions of The Global Nature of the Church.* 1999: GCCUIC. Also published in Dennis Campbell, William B. Lawrence, and Russell Richey, *Questions for the 21st Century Church,* Abingdon Press, 1999.

2. The World Methodist Council Handbook (2001–2006) lists seventy-seven churches, but it counts the UMC six times by dividing it into regions.

3. *The American Heritage® Dictionary of the English Language,* Fourth Edition Copyright © 2000 by Houghton Mifflin Company. Published by Houghton Mifflin Company.

4. I am using statistics compiled by David. B. Barrett and Todd M. Jonson. They report that, as of mid-2003, 1.097 billion Christians are Roman Catholic (out of 2.076 billion Christians). *International Bulletin of Missionary Research,* Vol. 27, No. 1, January 2003.

5. Uppsala, 1968, as quoted in the Report of the Moderator (Aram I), Central Committee, August 2002.

6. The latest statistics list 8,333,700 lay members in the jurisdictions listed in the United States and 1.5 million lay members in the Central Conferences. However, if the statistics counted members from baptism, the numbers would be considerably larger.

7. Statistics from David Barrett's *Status of Global Mission, 2001. International Bulletin of Missionary Research,* January 2001.

8. Historically, a "branch theory" of ecclesiology emerged within the Anglican tradition in the late sixteenth century. In a statement on church relations published by the Holy Synod of the Russian Orthodox Church in 2000, the branch theory was described as an ecumenical heresy since it presumes a dividedness of "the one holy catholic and apostolic church."

9. These questions were posed at the 2001 Central Committee meeting in the *Report of the General Secretary.* They were also placed in the WCC Final *Report of the Special Commission on Orthodox Participation in the WCC,* WCC Central Committee, 2002.

Chapter Three

1. Bishop William Boyd Grove, later President of the General Commission on Christian Unity and Interreligious Concerns and Ecumenical Officer of the

Council of Bishops, submitted an amendment to the proposal for the World Methodist Structure Conference "acknowledging the priority of the commitment of the UMC to the pursuit of unity with Christians of other churches both in the United States and throughout the world" (p. 250).

Chapter Four

1. Within the African Methodist Church there is a movement underway to change this practice and elect bishops locally in those areas.

2. Unfortunately, the definitions in the *Book of Discipline* are unhelpful since they do not make the adequate distinction between an "autonomous Methodist Church" or an "affiliated autonomous Methodist Church." The GCCUIC hopes to address this confusion at the 2004 General Conference. The present language leaves no room for a Methodist church that did not emerge from the UMC or one of its constituent members (¶ 546.1 and 547).

3. See Bruce Marshall, *"Who Really Cares About Christian Unity?" First Things,* January 2001, pp. 29-34.

4. Central Conferences do pay a portion of the support for bishops that are elected and serve wtihin their own central conferences. Technically, the money is paid to the General Episcopal Fund and then is returned to the conference. If need be (and as is often the case), the portion the annual conference is able to pay is supplemented by additional monies from the General Episcopal Fund that do not come from the annual conference (¶ 537.4).

5. The transitions in patterns of support to autonomous affiliated churches and to other ecumenical projects make this subject particularly sensitive. Historically, the General Board of Global Ministries has made few distinctions in its support of partners through grants and "advance" gifts. With the diminution of funding they are under greater pressure to prefer UM projects. Also, there is concern when non-UM projects solicit support within annual conferences in competition with UM projects.

6. There had been many years of contact between United Methodists from across the world and United Methodists who moved to Zimbabwe, many of them as miners.

7. There are also examples reported of expansion of the Methodist Church of Southern Africa into Angola and Mozambique, areas traditionally part of the United Methodist Church mission development.

8. The Africa Central Conferences have had a published *Book of Discipline.* I do not know whether it provides a significant connection to other United Methodists and to what extent it contextualizes the United Methodist polity or social perspective.

9. Research has shown that Methodists were involved in Russia during different periods, such as prior to the Russian revolution and in the years of Soviet control. This history has challenged the argument put forward by the Russian Orthodox Church that the UMC is a "new" church (sometimes called a sect) in Russia.

10. At present, *The Book of Discipline 2000* forbids new concordats from including the right of vote at General Conference (¶ 552.4a). However, such a prohibition may be illegal in light of the constitution's permission for concordat churches to vote given in ¶ 12.2.